THE HEAD VOICE
OTHER PROBLEMS
PRACTICAL TALKS
ON SINGING
BY
D. A. CLIPPINGER

INTRODUCTION

The following chapters are the outgrowth of an enthusiasm for the work of voice training, together with a deep personal interest in a large number of conscientious young men and women who have gone out of my studio into the world to engage in the responsible work of voice teaching.

The desire to be of service to them has prompted me to put in permanent form the principles on which I labored, more or less patiently, to ground them during a course of three, four, or five years. The fact that after having stood the "grind" for that length of time they are still asking, not to say clamoring, for more, may, in a measure, justify the decision to issue this book. It is not an arraignment of vocal teachers, although there are occasional hints, public and private, which lead me to believe that we are not altogether without sin. But if this be true we take refuge in the belief that our iniquity is not inborn, but rather is it the result of the educational methods of those immediately preceding us. This at least shifts the responsibility.

Words are dangerous things, and are liable at any moment to start a verbal conflagration difficult to control. Nowhere is this more likely to occur than in a discussion of voice training.

From a rather wide acquaintance with what has been said on this subject in the past hundred years, I feel perfectly safe in submitting the proposition that the human mind can believe anything and be conscientious in it.

Things which have the approval of ages emit the odor of sanctity, and whoever scoffs does so at his peril. Charles Lamb was once criticised for speaking disrespectfully of the equator, and a noted divine was severely taken to task for making unkind remarks about hell. Humanity insists that these time honored institutions be treated with due respect. I have an equal respect for those who believe as I do and those who do not; therefore if anything in this book is not in accord with popular opinion it is a crack at the head of the idol rather than that of the worshipper.

There is no legislative enactment in this great and free country to prevent us from *believing* anything we like, but there vshould be some crumbs of comfort in the reflection that we cannot *know* anything but the truth. One may believe that eight and three are thirteen if it please him, but he cannot know it because it is not true. Everything that is true has for its basis certain facts, principles, laws, and these are eternal and unchangeable. The instant the law governing any particular thing becomes definitely known, that moment it becomes undebatable. All argument is eliminated; but while we are searching for these laws we are dealing largely in opinions, and here the offense enters, for as Mr. Epictetus once said, "Men become offended at their opinion of things, not at the things themselves." We can scarcely imagine any one taking offense at the multiplication table, neither is this interesting page from the arithmetic any longer considered a fit subject for debate in polite society, but so far as we know this is the only thing that is immune.

Our musical judgments, which are our opinions, are governed by our experience; and with the growth of experience they ripen into solid convictions. For many years I have had a conviction that voice training is much simpler and less involved than it is generally considered. I am convinced that far too much is made of the vocal mechanism, which under normal conditions always responds automatically. Beautiful tone should be the primary aim of all voice teaching, and more care should be given to forming the student's tone concept than to that of teaching him how to control his throat by direct effort. The controlling power of a right idea is still much underestimated. The scientific plan of controlling the voice by means of mechanical directions leaves untouched the one thing which prevents its normal, automatic action, namely tension.

But, someone inquires, "If the student is singing with rigid throat and tongue would you say nothing about it?" I would correct it, but not by telling him to hold his tongue down. A relaxed tongue is always in the right place, therefore all he needs to learn about the tongue is how to relax it.

It has been hinted that he who subscribes to Dr. Fillebrown's declaration that ** *Resonance in Singing and Speaking*, by Thomas Fillebrown."The process of singing is psychologic rather than physiologic" has nothing tangible to work with. Now tone concept and musical feeling are absolutely essential to singing, and they are definite entities to one who has them. All musical temperaments must be vitalized. Imaginations vimust be trained until they will burst into flame at the slightest poetic suggestion. Musical natures are not fixed quantities. They are all subject to the law of growth. Every vocal student is an example of the law of evolution. Few people find it easy in the beginning to assume instantly a state of intense emotion. These things are habits of mind which must be developed, and they furnish the teacher with definite problems.

To repeat, *the tone is the thing*, and *how it sounds* is what determines whether it is right or wrong. And so we come back again to the ear, which is the taste. Does it please the ear? If so, is the ear reliable? Not always. If all teachers were trying for the same tone quality there would be no need of further writing on the subject, but they are not. On the contrary no two of them are trying for exactly the same quality. Each one is trying to make the voice produce his idea of tone quality, and the astounding thing about the human voice is that for a time at least, it can approximate almost anything that is demanded of it. If a voice is ruined, the ear of the teacher is directly responsible. It is useless to try to place the blame elsewhere.

Truth is always simple. If it seems difficult it is due to our clumsy way of stating it. Thought, like melodies, should run on the line of the least resistance. In the following pages I have eschewed all mystifying polysyllabic verbiage, and as Mark Twain once said, have "confined myself to a categorical statement of facts unincumbered by an obscuring accumulation of metaphor and allegory."

It is hoped that this book will be useful. It is offered as a guide rather than as a reformer. It aims to point in the right direction, and "do its bit" in emphasizing those things which are fundamental in voice training. Whatever is true in it will reach and help those who need it. Nothing more could be asked or desired.

Kimball Hall, Chicago.
May, 1917.

I

VOICE PLACING

"The path of the sound, being formed of elastic and movable parts, varies its dimensions and forms in endless ways, and every modification—even the slightest—has a corresponding and definite influence on the voice."

Garcia. Hints on Singing.

Vocal teachers are rated primarily on their ability as voice builders. When students look for a teacher the first thing they want to know is: "Can he build a voice?" His ability as an interpreter in most instances is taken for granted. Why this is so is easily understood. There is a moving appeal in the pure singing tone of the human voice that cannot even be approximated by any other instrument. We have all heard voices that were so beautiful that to hear one of them vocalize for half an hour would be a musical feast. Such a voice is so full of feeling, so vibrant with life and emotion that it moves one to the depths even if no words are used. It is only natural that all singers should be eager to possess such a voice, for it covers up a multitude of other musical misdemeanors. While it does not take the place altogether of the interpretative instinct, it does make the work of the singer much easier by putting his audience in sympathy with him from the beginning, thus to a considerable extent disarming criticism. The old Italians attached so much importance to beautiful tone that they were willing to work conscientiously for half a dozen years to obtain it. To the beautiful tone they added a faultless technic. Altogether it required from five to eight years to 2prepare and equip a singer for a career, but when he was thus prepared he could do astounding things in the way of trills, roulades, and cadenzas.

The stories of many of these singers have come down to us through the musical histories, and the singing world has come to believe that the teachers alone were responsible. Owing to her geographic location, her climate, language, and racial characteristics Italy at one time furnished most of the great singers of the world, and the world with its usual lack of judgment and discrimination gave Italian teachers all of the credit. That the best of the Italian teachers were as near right as it is humanly possible to be, I have no doubt whatever, but along with the few singers who became famous there were hundreds who worked equally hard but were never heard of. A great voice is a gift of the creator, and the greater the gift the less there is to be done by the teacher. But in addition to what nature has done there is always much to be done by the teacher, and the nature of the vocal instrument is such that its training is a problem unique and peculiar. The voice can do so many different things, produce so many different kinds of tone, in such a variety of ways that the ability to determine which is right and which is wrong becomes a matter of aesthetic judgment rather than scientific or mechanical.

If the scale, power, quality, and compass of the human voice were established as are those of the piano, the great problem in the training of a singer would be much simplified, possibly eliminated; but the singer must form the pitch, power, and quality of each tone as he uses it; therefore in the training of a singer we are constantly facing what has crystallized into the term **Voice Placing**.

This term has been used as a peg upon which to hang every whim, fancy, formula, and vocal vagary that has floated through the human mind in the last two centuries. It has furnished 3an excuse for inflicting upon vocal students every possible product of the imagination, normal and abnormal, disguised in the word **Method**, and the willingness with which students submit themselves as subjects for experiment is beyond belief. The more mysterious and abnormal the process the more faith they have in its efficacy.

2

The nature of the vocal instrument, its wide range of possibilities, and its intimate relation to the imagination make it a peculiarly fit subject for experiment. The scientist has tried to analyze it, the mechanic has tried to make it do a thousand things nature never intended it to do, the reformer has tried to reform both, and the psychologist, nearest right of all, has attempted to remove it from the realm of the material altogether. There seems to be no way to stop this theorizing, and it doubtless will continue until the general musical intelligence reaches such a point that it automatically becomes impossible.

We are constantly hearing such remarks as "Mr. S knows how to place the voice." "Mr. G does not." "Mr. B places the voice high." "Mr. R does not place the voice high enough." "Mr. X is great at bringing the tone forward," etc., etc. This goes on through a long list of fragments of English difficult to explain even by those who use them.

Now voice placing means just one thing, not half a dozen. It means learning to produce **beautiful tone**. When one can produce beautiful tone throughout his vocal compass his voice is placed, and it is not placed until he can. The injunction to *place the voice* invariably leaves in the mind of the student the idea that he must direct the tone to some particular point, in fact he is often urged to do so, whereas the truth is that when the tone is properly produced there is no thought of trying to put it anywhere. It seems to sing itself. There is a well established belief among students that the tone must 4be consciously directed to the point where it is supposed to focus. This belief is intimately associated with another equally erroneous, that the only way to tell whether a tone is good or bad, right or wrong, is by the way it feels. A tone is something to hear. It makes its appeal to the ear, and why one should rely on the sense of feeling to tell whether it sounds right or wrong is something difficult to understand.

Further, explicit directions are given for the action and control of everything involved in making tone except the mind of the student. The larynx seems to be particularly vulnerable and is subject to continuous attack. One says it should be held low throughout the compass. Another says it should rise as the pitch rises, and still another, that it should drop as the pitch rises. Instructions of this kind do not enlighten, they mystify.

If there be any one thing upon which voice teachers theoretically agree it is "free throat". Even those who argue for a fixed larynx agree to this, notwithstanding it is a physical impossibility to hold the larynx in a fixed position throughout the compass without a considerable amount of rigidity. It is like believing in Infinite Love and eternal punishment at the same time.

When the larynx is free it will not and should not be in the same position at all times. It will be a little lower for somber tones than for bright tones. It will be a little higher for the vowel e than for oo or o, but the adjustments will be *automatic*, never conscious. It cannot be too often reiterated that every part of the vocal mechanism must act automatically, and it is not properly controlled until it does.

The soft palate also comes in for its share of instruction. I was once taught to raise it until the uvula disappeared. Later I was taught to relax it. Both of these movements of the soft palate were expected to result in a beautiful tone. Now if 5two things which are directly opposed to each other are equal to the same thing, then there is no use in bothering our heads further with logic.

Such directions I believe to be of doubtful value, if not irrelevant. We must learn that *an idea has definite form*, and that when the mechanism is free, that is, plastic, the idea molds it into a corresponding form and the expression becomes a perfect picture of the idea. This is what is meant by indirect control, involuntary, automatic action.

One could write indefinitely on the peculiarities of voice training, the unique suggestions made, the mechanical instructions given, the unbelievable things students are made to do with lips, tongue and larynx as a necessary preparation to voice production. In this as in everything else there are extremists. Some have such an exquisite sense of detail that they never get beyond it. At the other extreme are those who trust everything to take care of itself. Both overlook the most important thing, namely, how the voice sounds.

It requires much time, study and experience to learn that voice training is simple. It is a fact that truth is naturally, inherently simple. Its mastery lies in removing those things which seem to make it difficult and complex. Training the voice, this so called "voice placing," is simple and easy when one has risen above that overwhelming amount of fiction, falsity, and fallacy that has accumulated around it, obscuring the truth and causing many well intentioned teachers to follow theories and vagaries that have no foundation in fact, and which lead both teacher and pupil astray. If there is any truth applicable to voice training it has an underlying principle, for truth is the operation of principle. If we start wrong we shall end wrong. If we start right and continue according to principle we shall reach the desired goal.

Voice training has its starting point, its basis, its 6foundation, in beautiful tone. This should be the aim of both teacher and pupil from the beginning. To produce something beautiful is the aim of all artistic activity. Beautiful tone, as Whistler said of all art, has its origin in absolute truth. That which is not beautiful cannot possibly be true, for real nature, which is the expression of Infinite Mind, is always perfect, and no perfect thing can be ugly, discordant, or inharmonious. The imperfection we see is the result of our own imperfect understanding of the real universe.

A tone is something to hear, and **hearing is mental.** An old French anatomist once said: "The eye sees what it is looking for, and it is looking only for what it has in mind." The same is true of the ear. We hear the tone mentally before we sing it, and we should hear it as distinctly as if it were sung by another. A tone first of all is a mental product, and its pitch, power, and quality are definite mental entities. When we wish to convey this tone to another we do it through the sound producing instrument which nature has provided for this purpose.

That everything exists first as idea has been the teaching of the philosophers for ages. That the idea is the controlling, governing force is equally well understood. Therefore, inasmuch as the aim of all voice building is to produce beautiful tone we must start with the right idea of tone. This is where the first and greatest difficulty appears. To most people a tone is intangible and difficult to define. One will rarely find a student that can formulate anything approaching a definition of a musical tone and I fancy many teachers would find it far from easy. Unless one has a grasp of the psychology of voice, and a great many have not, he will begin to work with what he can see. Here enters the long dreary mechanical grind that eventually ruins the temper of both teacher and student, and⁷results in nothing but mechanical singing, instead of a joyous, inspiring musical performance.

In studying the pure singing tone we find the following: It is *smooth, steady, firm, rich, resonant, sympathetic.* We shall also find that all of its qualities and attributes are mental. It must contain the element of freedom (mental), firmness (mental), security (mental), sympathy (mental), enthusiasm, sentiment, joy, compassion, pity, love, sorrow (all mental). These are all qualities of the singing tone. They are not intangible. On the contrary, to the one who has them they are definite and are the things he works for from the beginning. They are basic and fundamental. All are combined in what I call *tone concept*, which is another word for musical ear, or musical taste. This tone concept is by far the most important thing in voice training. The student will not sing a tone better than the one he conceives mentally, therefore the mental concept of tone, or tone concept must be the basis of voice placing.

This tone concept, or mental picture of tone qualities controls the vocal instrument by indirection. True tone color does not come as the result of trying by some physical process to make the tone light or dark, but *from the automatic response to musical concept or feeling.*

In leaving this subject I wish to pay my respects to that company of cheerful sinners—the open throat propagandists. I was taught in my youth that the punishment for a sin committed ignorantly was none the less pungent and penetrating, and I trust that in administering justice to these offenders the powers will be prompt, punctilious and persevering. It is a worthy activity.

No mistake of greater magnitude was ever made since voice training began than that of holding the throat open by direct effort. It never resulted in a tone a real musician's ear could 8endure, nevertheless during the latter part of the nineteenth century and even the early part of the twentieth it was made such an integral part of voice culture that it seemed to be incorporated in the law of heredity, and vocal students, even before they were commanded, would try to make a large cavity in the back of the throat. I believe however, that there is much less of this than formerly. Vocal teachers are beginning to see that the one important thing is a free throat and that when this is gained the response of the mechanism to the mental demand is automatic and unerring.

9

II
THE HEAD VOICE

Let him take care, however, that the higher the notes, the more it is necessary to touch them with softness, to avoid screaming.

Tosi. (1647-1727) *Observations on Florid Song.*

That the development of the upper, or head voice, is the most difficult as well as the most important part of the training of the singing voice, will be readily admitted by every experienced singing teacher.

That the upper voice should be produced with as much comfort as the middle or lower, is scarcely debatable.

That a majority of singers produce their upper voice with more or less difficulty, need not be argued.

4

Why is it that after two, three or more years of study so many upper voices are still thick, harsh and unsteady?

There is nothing in the tone world so beautiful as the male or female head voice when properly produced, and there is nothing so excruciatingly distressing as the same voice when badly produced.

The pure head voice is unique in its beauty. It is full of freedom, elasticity, spiritual exaltation. It seems to float, as it were, in the upper air without connection with a human throat. Its charm is irresistible. It is a joy alike to the singer and the listener. It is the most important part of any singer's equipment. Why is it so difficult and why do so few have it? Various reasons are at hand.

The spirit of American enterprise has found its way into voice teaching. It is in the blood of both teacher and pupil. The slogan is "Put it over." This calls for big tone and they do not see why they should not have it at once.

10The ability to use the full power of the upper voice when occasion demands is necessary and right, but merely to be able to sing high and loud means nothing. All that is required for that is a strong physique and determination. Such voice building requires but little time and no musical sense whatever; but to be able to sing the upper register with full power, emotional intensity, musical quality and ease, is the result of long and careful work under the ear of a teacher whose sense of tone quality is so refined that it will detect instantly the slightest degree of resistance and not allow it to continue.

The ambitious young singer who has been told by the village oracle that she has a great voice and all she needs is a little "finishing," balks at the idea of devoting three or four years to the process, and so she looks for some one who will do it quickly and she always succeeds in finding him. To do this work correctly the old Italians insisted on from five to eight years with an hour lesson each day. To take such a course following the modern plan of one or two half hours a week, would have the student treading on the heels of Methuselah before it was completed.

It is not always easy to make students understand that the training of the voice means the development of the musical mentality and at best is never a short process. To most of them voice culture is a physical process and as they are physically fit, why wait?

Now the fact is that there is nothing physical in voice production save the instrument, and a strong physique has no more to do with good singing than it has with good piano playing. Voice production is a mental phenomenon. It is mentality of the singer impressing itself on the vocal instrument and expressing itself through it. The idea that the vocal instrument alone without mental guidance will produce beautiful tone is as fallacious as that a grand piano will produce 11good music whether the one at the keyboard knows how to play it or not.

Let it be understood once for all that *it is the mentality of the individual, not his body, that is musical or unmusical*. Both teacher and student must learn that there is much more to do mentally and much less to do physically than most people suspect. They must learn that a musical mentality is no less definite than a physical body, and is at least equally important; also that right thinking is as necessary to good voice production as it is to mathematics.

At this point there will doubtless be a strenuous objection from those who assert that tone cannot be produced without effort, and that a considerable amount of it is necessary, especially in the upper voice.

It will be readily admitted that the application of force is required to produce tone, but how much force? Certainly not that extreme physical effort that makes the singer red in the face and causes his upper tones to shriek rather than sing. Such a display of force discloses an erroneous idea of how to produce the upper voice. When there is the right relation existing between the breath and the vocal instrument, when there is the proper poise and balance of parts, no such effort is necessary. On the contrary the tone seems to flow and the effort required is only that of a light and pleasant physical exercise.

The pianist does not have to strike the upper tones any harder than the lower ones in order to bring out their full power. Why should the upper part of the voice require such prodigious effort?

Now *all voices should have a head register*. It is a part of nature's equipment, and this calls for a word on the classification of voices. It ought not to be difficult to determine whether a voice is soprano, alto, tenor, baritone or bass, but I find each year a considerable number that have been misled. Why? 12A number of things are responsible. One of the most common is that of mistaking a soprano who has a chest register for an alto. This singer finds the low register easier to sing than the upper, consequently she and her friends decide she is an alto. Thereafter she sings low songs and takes the alto part in the choir. The longer she follows this plan the less upper voice she will have, and when she goes to a teacher, unless he has a discriminating and analytical ear, he will allow her to remain in the alto class. There is always something in the fiber of a tone, even though it be badly produced, that will disclose to the trained ear what it will be when rightly produced.

Again, the human voice can produce such a variety of tone qualities that sometimes a soprano will cultivate a somber style of singing and a majority of people will call her alto. It requires a trained ear to detect what she is doing. The baritone also, because he often sings the bass part in a quartet, tries to make himself sound like a bass; this he does by singing with a somber, hollow quality which has little or no carrying power.

Another mistake is that of classifying a voice according to its compass. This is the least reliable method of all. The mere fact of having high tones does not necessarily make one a soprano, neither is a voice always to be classified as alto by reason of not being able to sing high. It is *quality* that decides what a voice is. Soprano is a quality. Alto is a quality. The terms tenor, baritone, bass, refer to a quality rather than a compass. These qualities are determined primarily by the construction of the organ.

But when voices are properly trained there is not so much difference in the compass as most people suppose. For example: the female head voice lies approximately within this compass 13and altos who learn to use the real head voice will have no difficulty in vocalizing that high.

At the lower end of the voice sopranos who have a chest register will often sing as low as most altos. But whether they sing high or low it is always the quality that determines the classification of the voice.

Many lyric sopranos have no chest register, and it would be a mistake to attempt to develop one. In such voices, which rarely have anything below middle C, the middle register must be strengthened and carried down and made to take the place of the chest voice.

It must not be understood that there is but one soprano quality, one alto quality, etc. The voice is so individual that it cannot be thus limited. There are many soprano qualities between the coloratura and the dramatic, and the same is true of alto, tenor, baritone and bass.

When the voice is rightly produced, its natural quality will invariably appear, and there it must be allowed to remain. An attempt to change it always means disaster.

It will be observed that the piano string diminishes in length and thickness as the pitch rises, and the voice must do something which corresponds to this. Otherwise it will be doing that which approximates stretching the middle C string, for example, until it will produce its octave.

In discussing the head voice it is the purpose to avoid as much as possible the mechanical construction of the instrument. This may be learned from the numerous books on the anatomy and physiology of the voice. It is an interesting subject, but beyond an elementary knowledge it is of little value to the teacher. A correct knowledge of how to train the voice must be gained in the studio, not in the laboratory. Its basis is the musical sense rather than the mechanical or scientific. All of the scientific or mechanical knowledge that 14the world has to offer is no preparation for voice training. A knowledge of the art of teaching begins when the teacher takes his first pupil, not before. Therefore the aim shall be to present the subject as it appears to the teacher.

We hear much of the value of vocal physiology as a guide to good voice production. It is also claimed that a knowledge of it will prevent the singer from misusing his voice and at the same time act as a panacea for vocal ills. These statements do not possess a single element of truth. The only way the singer can injure the vocal instrument is by forcing it. That is, by setting up a resistance in the vocal cords that prevents their normal action. If this is persevered in it soon becomes a habit which results in chronic congestion. Singing becomes increasingly difficult, especially in the upper voice, and in course of time the singer discovers that he has laryngitis. Will a knowledge of vocal physiology cure laryngitis? Never. Will it prevent any one from singing "throaty?" There is no instance of the kind on record. In a majority of cases laryngitis and other vocal ills are the direct results of bad voice production and disappear as the singer learns to produce his upper tones without resistance. These things are effects, not causes, and to destroy the effect we must remove the cause. This will be found to be a wrong habit and habits are mental, not physical. When a mental impulse and its consequent response become simultaneous and automatic the result is a habit, but it is the mental impulse that has become automatic.

The terms, *tension, rigidity, interference, resistance,* all mean essentially the same thing. They mean the various forms of contraction in the vocal instrument which prevents its involuntary action. If we follow these things back far enough we shall find that they all have their origin in some degree of fear. This fear, of which anxiety is a mild form, begins to show itself whenever the singer attempts tones above the compass of his15speaking voice. Here is undeveloped territory. The tone lacks power, quality and freedom, and as power is what the untrained singer always seeks first, he begins to force it. In a short time he has a rigid throat, and the longer he sings the more rigid it becomes. By the time he decides to go to a teacher his voice is in such a condition that he must take his upper tones with a thick, throaty quality or with a light falsetto.

Among female voices I have seen many that could sing nothing but a full tone in the upper register, and that only with an unsteady, unsympathetic quality.

Now a point upon which all voice teachers can agree is that the upper voice is not properly trained until it has a perfect *messa di voce* that is, until the singer can swell the tone from the lightest pianissimo to full voice and return, on any tone in his compass, without a break and without sacrificing the pure singing quality. How shall this be accomplished? If the singer is forcing the upper voice it is safe to say in the beginning that it never can be done by practicing with full voice. Such practice will only fasten the habit of resistance more firmly upon the singer. To argue in the affirmative is equivalent to saying that the continued practice of a bad tone will eventually produce a good tone.

There is but one way to the solution of the problem; the singer must get rid of resistance. When he has succeeded in doing that the problem of the head voice is solved. The bugaboo of voice placing permanently disappears. The difficulty so many have in placing the upper voice lies in this, that they try to do it without removing the one thing which prevents them from doing it. When the voice is free from resistance it places itself, that is, it produces without effort whatever quality the singer desires. The term "head voice," doubtless grew out of the sensation in the head which accompanies the upper tones, and this sensation is the result of the vibration of the air in 16the air head cavities. Many have taken this sensation as a guide to the production of the head voice, and in order to make sure of it they instruct the student to direct the tone into the head. This is not only an uncertain and unnecessary procedure, but is almost sure to develop a resistance which effectually prevents the tone from reaching the head cavities. When there is no interference the tone runs naturally into the proper channel. It is not necessary to use force to put it there.

HEAD RESONANCE

Whether or not the head cavities act as resonators is one of the many mooted points in voice training. Those who believe they do are much in the majority, but those in the minority are equally confident they do not. What are the arguments? That there is a sensation in the head cavities when singing in the upper part of the compass no one can deny. Does it affect tone quality? The minority offers the argument that it cannot do so because the soft palate automatically rises in singing a high tone, thus closing the passage through the nose. On the other side it is argued, and rightly, that the soft palate can be trained to remain low in singing high tones. But whether the soft palate is high or low does not settle the matter. It is not at all necessary that breath should pass through the nasal cavities in order to make them act as resonators. In fact it is necessary that it should not. It is the air that is already in the cavities that vibrates. All who are acquainted with resonating tubes understand this. Neither is it necessary that the vibrations should be transmitted to the head cavities by way of the pharynx and over the soft palate. They may be transmitted through the bones of the head. John Howard proved this, to his satisfaction at least, many years ago.

17I recall that in working with Emil Behnke he used an exercise to raise the soft palate and completely close the channel, yet no one can deny that his pupils had head resonance. There are certain facts in connection with this that are hard to side-step. Plunket Greene once told me that at one time he lost the resonance in the upper part of his voice, and on consulting a specialist he found a considerable growth on the septum. He had it removed and at once the resonance returned. Other equally strong arguments could be offered in support of the claim that the head cavities do act as resonators. At any rate the high or low palate is not the deciding factor.

Too much cannot be said on the subject of interference, or resistance. So long as there is any of it in evidence it has its effect on tone quality. It is the result of tension, and tension is a mental impulse of a certain kind. Its antidote is relaxation, which is a mental impulse of an opposite nature. It is necessary for most singers to work at this until long after they think they have it.

In preparing the head voice the student must begin with a tone that is entirely free from resistance and build from that. In a large majority of voices it means practicing with a light, soft tone. A voice that cannot sing softly is not rightly produced. While the student is working for the freedom which will give him a good half voice he is preparing the conditions for a good full voice. The conditions are not right for the practice of full voice until the last vestige of resistance has disappeared. The light voice is as necessary to artistic success as the full voice. The singer must have both, but he must never sacrifice quality for power.

In the female voice the readjustments of the mechanism known as changes of register usually occur at about

18In many lyric soprano voices I have found the same readjustment at the B and C above the staff

I have also noted in many bass voices a similar change of adjustment at the E and F below the bass clef

It would seem therefore, that in a majority of voices until an even scale has been developed, that these readjustments appear at about the E and F and B and C throughout the vocal compass. The exceptions to this rule are so numerous however, that it can scarcely be called a rule. Some voices will have but one noticeable readjustment, and it may be any one of the three.

In some voices the changes are all imperceptible. In others, due to wrong usage, they are abrupt breaks. In every instance the teacher must give the voice what it needs to perfect an even scale. There should be no more evidence of register changes in the vocal scale than in the piano scale.

Leaving the lower two changes for the moment, let us consider the one at the upper E and F. This one is so common among sopranos that there are few who have not one, two, or three weak tones at this point. To avoid these weak tones many are taught to carry the thicker tones of the middle register up as far as they can force them in order to get the "big tone" which seems to be the sole aim of much modern voice teaching. The victims of this manner of teaching never use the real head voice, and one thing happens to them all. As time goes on the upper voice grows more and more difficult, the high tones disappear one by one, and at the time when they should be doing their best singing they find themselves vocal wrecks. Some of them change from soprano to alto and end by that route.

19Now these are not instances that appear at long intervals. They are in constant evidence and the number is surprisingly large. The cause is ignorance of how to treat the upper voice, together with an insane desire for a "big tone" and a lack of patience to await until it grows. The incredible thing is that there is a teacher living whose ear will tolerate such a thing.

Now there is a way to develop the head voice that gives the singer not only the full power of his upper voice, but makes it free, flexible and vibrant, a sympathetic quality, a perfect *messa di voce*, and enables him to sing indefinitely without tiring his voice. He must learn that it is possible to produce a full tone with a light mechanism. This is the natural way of producing the head voice. Further, the light mechanism must be carried far below the point where the so called change of register occurs.

Every voice should have a head register, and it may be developed in the following way. With altos and sopranos I start with this exercise

Altos should begin at A.

The student should neither feel nor hear the tone in the throat. Therefore he should begin with a soft *oo*. The throat should be free, lips relaxed but slightly forward. There should be no puckering of the lips for*oo*. The tone should seem to form itself around the lips, not in the throat. In the beginning the exercise must be practiced softly. No attempt must be made to increase the power, until the tone is well established in the light mechanism. When the *oo* can be sung softly and without resistance as high as E flat use the same exercise with *o*.

The next step is to blend this light mechanism with the heavier mechanism. It may be done in this way,

20Sing this descending scale with a crescendo, always beginning it *pp*. It should be practiced very slowly at first, and with portamento. Carrying the head voice down over the middle and the middle down over the lower will in a short time blend all parts of the voice, and lay the foundation of an even scale. The exercise should be transposed upward by half steps as the voice becomes more free until it reaches F or F sharp.

The next step is the building process. Use the following:

Altos should begin at A. In practicing these swells great care must be taken. Tone quality is the first consideration, and the tone must be pressed no further than is possible while retaining the pure singing quality. Where voices have been forced and are accustomed to sing nothing but thick tones this building process is sometimes slow. The student finds an almost irresistible tendency to increase the resistance as he increases the power of the tone. Therefore the louder he sings the worse it sounds. This kind of practice will never solve the problem. When the student is able to swell the tone to full power without increasing the resistance the problem is solved.

The progress of the student in this, as in everything in voice training, depends upon *the ear of the teacher*. The untrained ear of the student is an unreliable guide. The sensitive ear of the teacher must at all times be his guide. The belief that every one knows a good tone when he hears it has no foundation in fact. If the student's concept of tone were perfect he would not need a teacher. He would have the teacher within himself. Every one knows what he likes, and what he likes is of necessity his standard at that particular time, but it is only the measure of his taste and may be different the next day.

8

All things in voice training find their court of last resort in 21the ear of the teacher. All other knowledge is secondary to this. He may believe any number of things that are untrue about the voice, but if he have a thoroughly refined ear it will prevent him from doing anything wrong. His ear is his taste, his musical sense, and it is his musical sense, his musical judgment, that does the teaching.

So in building the head voice the teacher must see to it that musical quality is never sacrificed for power. A full tone is worse than useless, unless the quality is musical and this can never be accomplished until the vocal instrument is free from resistance.

Exercise No. 3 should be transposed upward by half steps, but never beyond the point at which it can be practiced comfortably.

As tension shows most in the upper part of the voice the student should have, as a part of his daily practice, exercises which release the voice as it rises. Use the following:

Begin with medium power and diminish to *pp* as indicated. The upper tone must not only be sung softly, but the throat must be entirely free. There must be no sense of holding the tone.

Transpose to the top of the voice.

No. 5 is for the same purpose as No. 4 but in an extended form. Begin with rather full voice and diminish to *pp* ascending. Increase to full voice descending. Continue the building of the upper voice using the complete scale.

22Thus far in preparing the head voice we have used the vowels *oo* and *o*. We may proceed to the vowel *ah* in the following way. Using Ex. No. 6 first sing *o* with loose but somewhat rounded lips. When this tone is well established sing *o* with the same quality, the same focus, or placing without rounding the lips. It amounts to singing *o* with the *ah* position. When this can be done then use short *u* as in the word *hum*. This gives approximately the placing for *ah* in the upper voice. When these vowels can all be sung with perfect freedom transpose upward by half steps.

In No. 7 when the crescendo has been made on the upper tone carry the full voice to the bottom of the scale.

This is another way of blending the different parts of the voice. It should be sung portamento in both directions. When sung by a female voice it will be Middle, Head, Middle as indicated by the letters M, H, M. When sung by the male voice it will be Chest, Head, Chest as indicated by the letters C, H, C. Transpose upward by half steps.

When the foregoing exercises are well in hand the head voice may be approached from the middle and lower registers in scale form as in the following:

23

The fact that male voices are more often throaty in the upper register then female voices calls for special comment.

The following diagram showing the relationship of the two voices will help to elucidate the matter.

I have here used three octaves of the vocal compass as sufficient for the illustration. Remembering that the male voice is an octave lower than the female voice we shall see that the female voice is a continuation, as it were, of the male voice; the lower part of the female compass overlapping the upper part of the male compass, the two having approximately an octave G to G in common. Further it will be seen that both male and female voices do about the same thing at the same absolute pitches. At about E flat or E above middle C the alto or soprano passes from the chest to the middle register. It is at the same absolute pitches that the tenor passes from what is usually called open to covered tone, but which might better be called from chest to head voice. There is every reason to believe24that the change in the mechanism is the same as that which occurs in the female voice at the same pitches. That there is oftentimes a noticeable readjustment of the mechanism in uncultivated voices at these pitches no observing teacher will deny, and these are the voices which are of special interest to the teacher, and the ones for which books are made. It will be observed that this change in the male voice takes place in the upper part of his compass instead of in the lower, as in the female voice. This change which is above the compass of the speaking voice of the tenor or baritone, adds greatly to its difficulty. For this reason the training of the male head voice requires more care and clearer judgment than anything else in voice training.

In treating this part of the female voice we have learned that if the heavy, or chest voice, is carried up to G or A above middle C it weakens the tones of the middle register until they finally become useless. Then the chest tones become more difficult and disappear one by one and the voice has no further value. Identically the same thing happens to the tenor who, by reason of

9

sufficient physical strength forces his chest voice up to G, A, or B flat. He may be able to continue this for awhile, sometimes for a few years, but gradually his upper tones become more difficult and finally impossible and another vocal wreck is added to the list.

In restoring the female voice that has carried the chest voice too high it is necessary to carry the middle register down, sometimes as low as middle C until it has regained its power. The tenor or baritone must do essentially the same thing. He must carry the head voice, which is a lighter mechanism than the chest voice, down as low as this c using what is often called mixed voice. When the pitches are practiced with a sufficiently relaxed 25throat the tone runs naturally into the head resonator with a feeling almost the equivalent of that of a nasal tone, but this tone will be in no sense nasal. It will be head voice.

THE FALSETTO

Does the falsetto have any part in the development of the head voice? This inoffensive thing is still the subject of a considerable amount of more of less inflammatory debate both as to what it is and what it does. Without delay let me assure every one that it is perfectly harmless. There is no other one thing involved in singing, immediate or remote, from which the element of harm is so completely eliminated. It is held by some that it is produced by the false vocal chords. This position is untenable for the reason that I have known many singers who could go from the falsetto to a full ringing tone and return with no perceptible break. Now since it will hardly be argued that a ringing, resonant tone could be produced by the false vocal cords, it is evident that the singer must change from the false to the true vocal cords somewhere in the process—a thing which is unthinkable.

It is held by others that the falsetto is a relic of the boy's voice, which has deteriorated from lack of use. This seems not unreasonable, and a considerable amount of evidence is offered in support of it. We may safely assume however that it is produced by the true vocal cords and the lightest register in the male voice. What is its use? Unless its quality can be changed it has little or no musical value. There are some teachers who claim that the falsetto mechanism is the correct one for the tenor voice and should be used throughout the entire compass. I am not prepared to subscribe to this. There are others who believe that the falsetto should be developed, 26resonated, so that it loses its flute quality, and blended with the head voice. This seems in the light of my experience to be reasonable. When this can be done it gives the singer the most perfect mechanism known. But it cannot always be done. The voice is individual, and the entire sum of individual experience leaves its impression on it. I have found many voices where the falsetto was so completely detached from the head voice that it would be a waste of time to attempt to blend them.

But there is one place in voice training where the practice of the falsetto has a distinct value. I have seen many tenors and baritones who forced the heavy chest voice up until they developed an automatic clutch, and could sing the upper tones only with extreme effort. To allow them to continue in that way would never solve their problem. In such a condition half voice is impossible. It must be one thing or the other, either the thick chest voice or falsetto. The falsetto they can produce without effort, and herein lies its value. They become accustomed to hearing their high tones without the association of effort, and after a time the real head voice appears. The thing which prevented the head voice from appearing in the beginning was extreme resistance, and as soon as the resistance disappeared the head voice made its appearance. This was accomplished by the practice of the very light register known as falsetto. When the head voice appears the use of the falsetto may be discontinued.

The thing expected of the teacher is results and he should not be afraid to use anything that will contribute to that end.

It is in the upper part of the voice that mistakes are most likely to be made and ninety nine per cent of the mistakes is forcing the voice, that is, singing with too much resistance. So long as the resistance continues a good full tone is impossible. The plan outlined above for eliminating resistance has been 27tested with many hundreds of voices and has never failed. The idea held by some that such practice can never produce a large tone shows a complete misunderstanding of the whole matter. That it produces the full power of the voice without sacrificing its musical quality is being proved constantly.

Every day we hear the story of voices ruined by forcing high tones. Who is responsible? Each one must answer for himself. With the hope of diminishing it in some degree, this outline is offered.

28

III
A GENERAL SURVEY OF THE SITUATION
"I will roar you as gently as any sucking dove: I will roar you an't were any nightingale."
Shakespeare. *A Midsummer Night's Dream.*

The singing world is confronted with a situation unique in its humor. On every side we hear the lachrymose lament that voice training is in a chaotic condition, that *bel canto* is a lost art, and that the golden age of song has vanished from the earth.

The unanimity of this dolorous admission would seem to be a sad commentary on the fraternity of voice teachers; but here enters the element of humor. There is not recorded a single instance of a voice teacher admitting that his own knowledge of the voice is chaotic. He will admit cheerfully and oftentimes with ill concealed enthusiasm that every other teacher's knowledge is in a chaotic condition, but his own is a model of order and intelligence.

If we accept what voice teachers think of themselves the future looks rosy. If we accept what they think of each other the future is ominous and the need for reform is dire and urgent.

But if a reform be ordered where shall it begin? Obviously among the teachers themselves. But judging from the estimate each one puts upon himself how shall we reform a thing which is already perfect? On the other hand, if we take the pessimistic attitude that all teachers are wrong will it not be a case of the blind leading the blind, in which instance their destination is definitely determined somewhere in the New Testament. Verily the situation is difficult. Nevertheless it is not altogether hopeless. The impulse to sing still remains. 29More people are studying singing, and more people sing well today than at any other time in the history of the world. The impulse to sing is as old as the human race. When the joy of life first welled up within man and demanded utterance the vocal instrument furnished by nature was ready to respond and the art of singing began, and if we may venture a prophecy it will never end in this world or the next. It cannot be destroyed even by the teachers themselves. It is this natural, inborn desire to sing that is directly responsible for the amazing perseverance of many vocal students. If after a year or two of study they find they are wrong they are not greatly disturbed, but select another teacher, firm in the faith that eventually they will find the right one and be safely led to the realization of their one great ambition—to be an artist. It is this that has kept the art alive through the centuries and will perpetuate it. This impulse to sing is something no amount of bad teaching can destroy.

THE REFORM

Everything in the universe that has come under the scrutiny of mortal man has been subjected to a perpetual reformation. Nothing is too great or too small to engage the attention of the reformer. Religion, politics, medicine and race suicide are objects of his special solicitude, but nothing else has been forgotten. No phase of human activity has been allowed to remain at rest. So far as we know nothing but the multiplication table has escaped the reformer. There is a general feeling that nothing is exactly right. This may be the operation of the law of progress, doubtless it is, but it occasions a mighty unrest, and keeps the world wondering what will happen next. This law of progress is but another name for idealism to which 30the world owes everything. Idealism is that which sees a better condition than the one which now obtains. The process of realizing this better condition is in itself reformation.

As far back as we have any knowledge of the art of singing the reformers have been at work, and down through the centuries their energies have been unflagging. We owe to them whatever advance has been made toward a perfect system of voice training, but they are also responsible for many things pernicious in their nature which have been incorporated in present day methods of teaching, for it must be admitted that there are false prophets among singing teachers no less than among the members of other professions. There is one interesting thing connected with the work of these vocal reformers. From the beginning they have insisted that the art of *bel canto* is lost. Tosi (1647-1727), Porpora (1686-1766), Mancini (1716-1800), three of the greatest teachers of the old Italian school, all lamented the decadence of the art of singing. Others before and since have done the same thing. It seems that in all times any one who could get the public ear has filled it with this sort of pessimistic wail. From this we draw some interesting conclusions: First, that the real art of singing was lost immediately after it was found. Second, that the only time it was perfect was when it began. Third, that ever since it began we have been searching for it without success. If any of this is true it means that all of the great singers of the past two hundred years have been fakers, because they never really learned how to sing. It is surprising that we did not see through these musical Jeremiahs long ago. In all ages there have been good teachers and bad ones, and it would not be surprising if the bad ones outnumbered the good ones; but the weak link in the chain of argument is in estimating the profession by its failures. This is a cheap and much overworked device and discloses the egotism of the one using 31it. There are teachers today who thoroughly understand the art of *bel canto*. They have not lost it, and the others never had it. This condition has obtained for centuries and will continue indefinitely. An art should be measured by its best exponents, not by its worst. To measure it by its failures is illogical and dishonest.

In recent years the process of reformation has been applied to all branches of music teaching with the hope of reducing these failures to a minimum. The profession has suddenly awakened to the fact that it must give a better reason for its existence than any heretofore offered. It has become clear to the professional mind that in order to retain and enlarge its self-respect music must be recognized as a part of the great human uplift. To this end it has been knocking at the doors of the institutions of learning asking to be admitted and recognized as a part of public education. The reply has been that music teaching must first develop coherence, system and standards. This has caused music teachers to look about and realize as never before that the profession as a whole has no organization and no fixed educational standards. Every teacher fixes his own standard and is a law unto himself. The standard is individual, and if the individual conscience is sufficiently elastic the standard gives him no serious concern. But as a result of this awakening there is a concerted action throughout the country to standardize, to define the general scope of learning necessary to become a music teacher. The trend of this is in the right direction, and good may be expected from it, although at best it can be but a very imperfect method of determining one's fitness to teach. The determining factors in teaching are things which cannot be discovered in any ten questions. In fact an examination must necessarily confine itself to general information, but in teaching, the real man reveals himself. His high sense of order, logic, patience, his love 32and appreciation of the beautiful, his personality, his moral sense, the mental atmosphere of his studio, these all enter into his teaching and they are things difficult to discover in an examination. Unconsciously the teacher gives out himself along with the music lesson, and it is equally important with his knowledge of music. Therefore it is as difficult to establish definite standards of teaching as it is of piano or violin making.

In attempting to establish standards of voice teaching the problem becomes positively bewildering. The voice is so completely and persistently individual, and in the very nature of things must always remain so, that an attempt to standardize it or those who train it is dangerous. Yet notwithstanding this, voice teachers are the most industrious of all in their efforts to organize and standardize. The insistence with which this aim is prosecuted is worthy of something better than is likely to be achieved.

That there is no standard among voice teachers save that of the individual will be admitted without argument; and until there is such a thing as a fixed standard of musical taste this condition will remain, for the musical taste of the teacher is by far the most potent factor in the teaching of tone production.

Of late there have been vigorous efforts to establish a standard tone for singers. This, according to the apostles of "Harmony in the ranks," is the one way of unifying the profession. As an argument this is nothing short of picturesque, and can be traced to those unique and professedly scientific mentalities that solve all vocal problems by a mathematical formula. As an example of the chimerical, impossible and altogether undesirable, it commands admiration. If it is impossible to establish a standard tone for pianos where the problem is mechanical, what may we expect to do with voice where the problem is psychological?

When we have succeeded in making all people look alike, 33act alike, think alike; when we have eliminated all racial characteristics and those resulting from environment; when people are all of the same size, weight, proportion, structure; when skulls are all of the same size, thickness and density; when all vocal organs and vocal cavities are of the same form and size; when we have succeeded in equalizing all temperaments; when there is but one climate, one language, one government, one religion; when there is no longer such a thing as individuality—then perhaps a standard tone may be considered. Until that time nothing could be more certain of failure. The great charm of voices is their individuality, which is the result not alone of training, but of ages of varied experience, for man is the sum of all that has preceded him. It is, to say the least, an extraordinary mentality that would destroy this most vital element in singing for the sake of working out a scientific theory.

But there is no immediate danger. Nature, whose chief joy is in variety and contrast, is not likely to sacrifice it suddenly to a mere whim.

When we speak of a standard tone we enter the domain of acoustics and must proceed according to the laws of physics. In this standard tone there must be a fundamental combined with certain overtones. But who shall say which overtones, and why the particular combination? The answer must be "because it sounds best." A tone being something to hear, this is a logical and legitimate answer. But if the listener knows when it sounds right he knows it entirely separate and apart from any knowledge he may have of its scientific construction; hence such knowledge is of no value whatever in determining what is good and what is bad in tone quality. A tone is not a thing to see and the teacher cannot use a camera and a manometric flame in teaching tone production. Any 34knowledge he may have gained from the use of such instruments in the laboratory is valueless in teaching.

If it were possible to adopt as a standard tone a certain combination of fundamental and overtones (which it is not), and if it were possible to make all singers use this particular tone (which, thank heaven it is not), then all voices would sound alike and individuality would at once disappear.

The advocates of this kind of standard tone cannot disengage themselves from the belief that all vocal organs are alike. The exact opposite is the truth. Vocal organs are no more alike than are eyes, noses, hands and dispositions. Each of these conforms only to a general type. The variation is infinite.

MENTALITY

The mentality of the individual forms the organ through which it can express itself, and this mentality is the accumulation of all of the experience which has preceded it. Further, muscles and cartilages are not all of the same texture. Thyroid cartilages vary in size and shape. The vocal cavities, pharynx, mouth and nasal cavities are never exactly the same in any two people. The contours of the upper and lower jaw and teeth, and of the palatal arch are never found to be exactly alike. All of these variations are a part of the vocal instrument and determine its quality. Every vocal organ when properly directed will produce the best quality of which that particular instrument is capable. An attempt to make it produce something else must necessarily be a failure. The structure of the instrument determines whether the voice is bass, tenor, alto or soprano with all of the variations of these four classes. The individuality of the voice is fixed by nature no less definitely.

35The effort to standardize tone quality discloses a misapprehension of what it means to train a voice. Its advocates look upon man as so much matter, and the voice as something which must be made to operate according to fixed mathematical rules and ignore completely its psychology.

But the rich humor of it all appears when the propagandists of standard tone meet to establish the standard. It is soon observed that there are as many standards as there are members present and the only result is a mental fermentation.

GETTING TOGETHER

In recent years many attempts have been made by vocal teachers to "get together." As nearly as can be ascertained this getting together means that all shall teach in the same way, that all shall agree on the disputed points in voice training, or that certain articles of faith to which all can subscribe, shall be formulated; but when it comes to deciding whose way it shall be or whose faith shall be thus exalted, each one is a Gibraltar and the only perceptible result is an enlargement of the individual ego. And so it endeth.

WHY TEACHERS DISAGREE

Voice teachers are divided into two general classes—those who make a knowledge of vocal physiology the basis of teaching and those who do not. The members of the first class follow the teachings of some one of the scientific investigators. Each one will follow the scientist or physiologist whose ideas most nearly coincide with his own, or which seem most reasonable to him. In as much as the scientists have not yet 36approached anything resembling an agreement, it follows that their disciples are far from being of one mind.

The members of the second class hold that a knowledge of vocal anatomy and physiology beyond the elements has no value in teaching, and that the less the student thinks about mechanism the better. The scientific voice teachers usually believe in direct control of the vocal organs. The members of the opposite class believe in indirect control. This establishes a permanent disagreement between the two general classes, but the disagreement between those who believe in indirect control is scarcely less marked. Here it is not so much a matter of how the tone is produced, but rather the tone itself. This is due entirely to the difference in taste among teachers. The diversity of taste regarding tone quality is even greater than that regarding meat and drink. This fact seems to be very generally overlooked. It is this that so mystifies students. After studying with a teacher for one or more years they go to another to find that he at once tries to get a different tone quality from that of the first. When they go to the third teacher he tries for still another quality. If they go to a half dozen teachers each one will try to make them produce a tone differing in some degree from all of the others. The student doubtless thinks this is due to the difference in understanding of the voice among teachers, but this is not so. It is due entirely to their differing tastes in tone quality. The marvelous thing is that the voice will respond in a degree to all of these different demands made upon it; but it forces the student to the conclusion that voice training is an indefinite something without order, system, or principle.

So, in studying the conditions which obtain in voice teaching at the present time it must be admitted that the evidence of unity is slight; and the probability of increasing it by organization or legislative enactment is not such as to make one enthusiastic. 37What one believes is very real to himself. In fact it is the only thing that seems right to him, therefore he sees no valid reason why he should change his belief or why others should not believe as he does.

13

This positive element in the human ego is advantageous at times, but it is also responsible for all conflicts from mild disagreements to war among nations.

But arguments and battles rarely ever result in anything more than an armed truce. Difference of opinion will continue indefinitely, but of this we may be sure, that the solution of the vocal problem will never come through a study of vocal mechanism however conscientious and thorough it may be, but through a purer musical thought, a deeper musical feeling, a clearer vision of what is cause and what is effect, a firmer conviction of the sanctity of music, an unerring knowledge of the relationship existing between the singer and his instrument.

38

IV

HINTS ON TEACHING

"We live in a world of unseen realities, the world of thoughts and feelings. But 'thoughts are things,' and frequently they weigh more and obtain far more in the making of a man than do all the tangible realities which surround him. Thoughts and feelings are the stuff of which life is made. They are the language of the soul. By means of them we follow the development of character, the shaping of the soul which is the one great purpose of life."

Appreciation of Art. Loveridge.

Every year a large number of young men and women go in quest of a singing teacher. The impulse to sing, which is inborn, has become so insistent and irrepressible that it must be heeded; and the desire to do things well, which is a part of the mental equipment of every normal human being, makes outside assistance imperative. Wherever there is a real need the supply is forthcoming, so there is little difficulty in finding some one who is ready, willing, in fact rather anxious, to undertake the pleasant task of transforming these enthusiastic amateurs into full-fledged professionals.

The meeting of the teacher and student always takes place in the studio, and it is there that all vocal problems are solved. Let no one imagine that any vocal problem can be solved in a physics laboratory. Why? *Because not one of the problems confronting the vocal student is physical. They are all mental.* The writer has reached this conclusion not from ignoring the physical, but from making a comprehensive study of the vocal mechanism and its relation to the singer.

The anatomy and physiology of the vocal mechanism are absorbing to one who is interested in knowing how man, through untold centuries of growth has perfected an instrument through which he can express himself; but no matter how far we go in the study of anatomy and physiology all we really 39learn is what mind has done. If man has a more perfect and highly organized vocal instrument than the lower animals it is because his higher manifestation of mind has formed an instrument necessary to its needs.

When man's ideas and needs were few and simple his vocabulary was small, for language is the means by which members of the species communicate with each other. Whenever man evolved a new idea he necessarily invented some way of communicating it, and so language grew. A word is the symbol of an idea, but invariably the idea originates the word. The word does not originate the idea. The idea always arrives first. All we can ever learn from the study of matter is phenomena, the result of the activity of mind.

Thus we see that so called "scientific study" of the vocal mechanism is at best, but a study of phenomena. It creates nothing. It only discovers what is already taking place, and what has been going on indefinitely without conscious direction will, in all probability, continue.

The value attached by some to the study of vocal physiology is greatly overestimated. In fact its value is so little as to be practically negligible. It furnishes the teacher nothing he can use in giving a singing lesson, unless, perchance he should be so unwise as to begin the lesson with a talk on vocal mechanism, which, by the way, would much better come at the last lesson than the first. All we can learn from the study of vocal physiology is the construction of the vocal instrument, and this bears the same relation to singing that piano making bears to piano playing. The singer and his instrument are two different things, and a knowledge of the latter exerts very little beneficial influence on the former.

To reach a solution of the vocal problem we must understand the relation existing between the singer and his instrument.

The singer is a mentality, consequently everything he does 40is an activity of his mentality. Seeing, hearing, knowing, is this mentality in action. The two senses most intimately associated with artistic activity are seeing and hearing, and these are mental. In painting, sculpture, and architecture we perceive beauty through the eye. In music it reaches us through the ear; but *the only thing that is cognizant is the mind.* To man the universe consists of mental impressions, and that these impressions differ with each individual is so well understood that it need not be argued. Two people looking at the same picture will not see exactly the same things. Two people listening to a musical composition may hear quite different things and are affected in different ways, because *it is the mind that hears*, and as no two mentalities are precisely the same, it must be apparent that the impressions they receive will be different. The things these mentalities have in common they will see and hear in common, but wherein they differ they will see and hear differently. Each will see and hear to the limit of his experience, but no further.

To be a musician one must become conscious of that particular thing called music. He must learn to think music. The elements of music are rhythm, melody, harmony, and form, and their mastery is no less a mental process than is the study of pure mathematics.

The human mind is a composite. It is made up of a large number of faculties combined in different proportions. The germs of all knowledge exist in some form and degree in every mind. When one faculty predominates we say the individual has talent for that particular thing. If the faculty is abnormally developed we say he is a genius, but all things exist as possibilities in every mind. Nature puts no limitations on man. Whatever his limitations, they are self imposed, nature is not a party to the act.

Now this is what confronts the teacher whenever a student 41comes for a lesson. He has before him a mentality that has been influenced not only by its present environment, but by everything that has preceded it. "Man is," as an old philosopher said, "a bundle of habits," and habits are mental trends. His point of view is the product of his experience, and it will be different from that of every one else. The work of the teacher is training this mentality. Understanding this it will be seen how futile would be a fixed formula for all students, and how necessarily doomed to failure is any method of voice training which makes anatomy and physiology its basis. Further, there is much to be done in the studio beside giving the voice lesson. Whistler said that natural conditions are never right for a perfect picture. From the picture which nature presents the artist selects what suits his purpose and rejects the rest. It is much the same in the training of a singer. In order that the lesson be effective the conditions must be right. This only rarely obtains in the beginning. The student's attitude toward the subject must be right or the lesson will mean little to him. The lesson to be effective must be protected by *honesty, industry* and*perseverance*. If these are lacking in various degrees, as they often are, little progress will be made. If the student is studying merely for "society purposes," not much can be expected until that mental attitude is changed. Students always want to sing well, but they are not always willing to make the sacrifice of time and effort; consequently they lack concentration and slight their practice. Sometimes the thought uppermost in the student's mind is the exaltation of the ego, in other words, fame. Sometimes he measures his efforts by the amount of money he thinks he may ultimately earn, be it great or small. Sometimes he overestimates himself, or what is equally bad, underestimates himself. It is a very common thing to find him putting limitations on himself and telling of the few things he will be able to do and the large number he 42never will be able to do, thus effectually barring his progress. Then there is always the one who is habitually late. She feels sure that all of the forces of nature are leagued in a conspiracy to prevent her from ever being on time anywhere. She, therefore, is guiltless. There is another one who is a riot of excuses, apologies and reasons why she has not been able to practice. Her home and neighborhood seem to be the special object of providential displeasure, which is manifested in an unbroken series of calamitous visitations ranging from croup to bubonic plague, each one making vocal practice a physical and moral impossibility.

All of these things are habits of mind which must be corrected by the teacher before satisfactory growth may be expected. In fact he must devote no inconsiderable part of his time to setting students right on things which in themselves are no part of music, but which are elements of character without which permanent success is impossible.

A great musical gift is of no value unless it is protected by those elements of character which are in themselves fundamentally right. Innumerable instances could be cited of gifted men and women who have failed utterly because their gifts were not protected by honesty, industry and perseverance.

I have spoken at some length of the importance of the right mental attitude toward study and the necessity of correcting false conceptions. Continuing, it must be understood that the work of the teacher is all that of training the mind of his student. It is developing concepts and habits of mind which when exercised result in beautiful tone and artistic singing. It must also be understood that the teacher does not look at the voice, he listens to it. Here voice teachers automatically separate themselves from each other. No two things so 43diametrically opposite as physics and metaphysics can abide peaceably in the same tent.

Let me emphasize the statement that *the teacher does not look at the voice, he listens to it.* The teacher who bases his teaching on what he can see, that is, on watching the singer and detecting his mistakes through the eye, is engaged in an activity that is mechanical, not musical. No one can tell from observation alone whether a tone is properly produced. A tone is something to hear, not something to see, and no amount of seeing will exert any beneficial influence on one's hearing.

The process of learning to read vocal music at sight is that of learning to *think tones*, to *think in the key*, and to *think all manner of intervals and rhythmic forms*. It is altogether mental, and it is no less absurd to hold that a knowledge of anatomy is necessary to this than it is essential to the solution of a mathematical problem. The formation of tone quality is no less a mental process than is thinking the pitch. If the student sings a wrong pitch it is because he has thought a wrong pitch, and this is true to a large extent at least, if his tone quality in not good. He may at least be sure of this, that *he never will sing a better tone than the one he thinks.*

A large part of the vocal teacher's training should be learning how to listen and what to listen for. This means training the ear, which is the mind, until it is in the highest degree sensitive to tone quality as well as to pitch. When there is a failure in voice training it may be counted upon that the teacher's listening faculty is defective. The gist of the whole thing is what the teacher's ear will stand for. If a tone does not offend his ear he will allow it to continue. If it does offend his ear he will take measures to stop it.

More is known of vocal mechanism today than at any other time in the world's history, and yet who dares to say that voice teaching has been improved by it? Is voice teaching any more 44accurate now than it was a hundred years ago? Did the invention of the laryngoscope add anything of value to the voice teacher's equipment? No. Even the inventor of it said that all it did was to confirm what he had always believed. An enlarged mechanical knowledge has availed nothing in the studio. The character of the teacher's work has improved to the degree in which he has recognized two facts—first, the necessity of developing his own artistic sense as well as that of his pupil, second, that the process of learning to sing is psychologic rather than physiologic.

When the student takes his first singing lesson what does the teacher hear? He hears the tone the student sings, but what is far more important, he hears in his own mind the tone the student ought to sing. He hears his own tone concept and this is the standard he sets for the student. He cannot demand of him anything beyond his own concept either in tone quality or interpretation.

Young teachers and some old ones watch the voice rather than listen to it. At the slightest deviation from their standard of what the tongue, larynx, and soft palate ought to do they pounce upon the student and insist that he make the offending organ assume the position and form which they think is necessary to produce a good tone. This results in trying to control the mechanism by direct effort which always induces tension and produces a hard, unsympathetic tone.

The blunder here is in mistaking effect for cause. The tongue which habitually rises and fills the cavity of the mouth does so in response to a wrong mental concept of cause. The only way to correct this condition is to change the cause. The rigid tongue we see is effect, and to tinker with the effect while the cause remains is unnecessarily stupid. An impulse of tension has been directed to the tongue so often that the impulse and response have become simultaneous and automatic. 45The correction lies in directing an impulse of relaxation to it. When it responds to this impulse it will be found to be lying in the bottom of the mouth, relaxed, and ready to respond to any demand that may be made upon it. To try to make the tongue lie in the bottom of the mouth by direct effort while it is filled with tension is like trying to sweep back the tide with a broom. The only way to keep the tide from flowing is to find out what causes it to flow and remove the cause. The only way to correct faulty action of any part of the vocal mechanism is to go back into mentality and remove the cause. It will always be found there.

DIRECT AND INDIRECT CONTROL

In view of the generally understood nature of involuntary action and the extent to which it obtains in all good singing it is difficult to understand why any teacher should work from the basis of direct control. It is a fact, however, that teachers who have not the psychological vision find it difficult to work with a thing they cannot see. To such, direct control seems to be the normal and scientific method of procedure.

Let me illustrate: A student comes for his first lesson. I "try his voice." His tone is harsh, white, throaty and unsympathetic. It is not the singing tone and I tell him it is "all wrong." He does not contradict me but places himself on the defensive and awaits developments. I question him to find out what he thinks of his own voice, how it impresses him, etc. I find it makes no impression on him because he has no standard. He says he doesn't know whether he ought to like his voice or not, but rather supposes he should not. As I watch him I discover many things that are wrong and I make a mental note of them. Suppose I say to him as a very celebrated European 46teacher once said to me: "Take a breath, and concentrate your mind on the nine little muscles in the throat that control the tone." This is asking a good deal when he does not know the name or the exact location of a single one of them, but he seems impressed, although a little perplexed, and to make it easier for him I say as another famous teacher once said to me: "Open your mouth, put two fingers and a thumb between your teeth, yawn, now sing *ah*." He makes a convulsive effort and the tone is a trifle worse than it was before. I say to him, "Your larynx is too high, and it jumps up at the beginning of each tone. You must keep it down. It is impossible to produce good tone with a high larynx. When the larynx rises, the throat closes and you must always have your throat open. Don't forget, your throat must be *open* and you can get it open only by keeping the larynx low." He tries again with the same result and awaits further instructions. I take another tack and say to him, "Your tongue rises every time you sing and impairs the form of the vocal cavity. Keep it down below the level of the teeth, otherwise your vowels will be imperfect. You should practice a half hour each day grooving your tongue." I say these things impressively and take the opportunity to tell him some interesting scientific facts about fundamental and upper partials, and how different combinations produce different vowels, also how these combinations are affected by different forms of the vocal cavities, leading up to the great scientific truth that he must hold the tongue down and the throat open in order that these great laws of acoustics may become operative. He seems very humble in the presence of such profound erudition and makes several unsuccessful attempts to do what I tell him, but his tone is no better. I tell him so, for I do not wish to mislead him. He is beginning to look helpless and discouraged but waits to see what I will do next. He vexes me not a little, because I feel that anything 47so simple and yet so scientific as the exercises I am giving him ought to be grasped and put into practice at once; but I still have resources, and I say to him, "Bring the tone forward, direct it against the hard palate just above the upper teeth, send it up through the head with a vigorous impulse of the diaphragm. You must always feels the tone in the nasal cavities. That is the way you can tell whether your tone is right or not." He tries to do these things, but of necessity fails.

This sort of thing goes on with mechanical instructions for raising the soft palate, making the diaphragm rigid, grooving the tongue, etc., etc., and at the end of the lesson I tell him to go home and practice an hour a day on what I have given him. If he obeys my instructions he will return in worse condition, for he will be strengthening the bad habits he already has and forming others equally pernicious.

This is a sample of teaching by direct control. It is not overdrawn. It is a chapter from real life, and I was the victim.

You will have observed that this lesson was devoted to teaching the student how to do certain things with the vocal mechanism. The real thing, the tone, the result at which all teaching should aim was placed in the background. It was equivalent to trying to teach him to do something but not letting him know what. It was training the body, not the mind, and the result was what invariably happens when this plan is followed.

In the lesson given above no attempt was made to give the student a correct mental picture of a tone, and yet this is the most important thing for him to learn, for *he never will sing a pure tone until he has a definite mental picture of it. A tone is something to hear and the singer himself must hear it before he can sing it.*

Not one of the suggestions made to this student could be of 48any possible benefit to him at the time. Not even the sensation of feeling the tone in the head can be relied upon, for physical sensations are altogether uncertain and unreliable. As I have observed in numberless instances, there may be a sensation in the head when there are disagreeable elements in the tone. If the ear of the teacher does not tell him when the tone is good and when it is bad he is hopeless. If his ear is reliable, why resort to a physical sensation as a means of deciding? In the properly produced voice there is a feeling of vibration in the head cavities, especially in the upper part of the voice, but that alone is not a guaranty of good tone.

This teaching from the standpoint of sensation and direct control will never produce a great singer so long as man inhabits a body. It is working from the wrong end of the proposition. Control of the mechanism is a very simple matter when the mental concept is formed. It is then only a question of learning how to relax, how to free the mechanism of tension, and the response becomes automatic.

Is there no way out of this maze of mechanical uncertainties? There is. Is voice culture a sort of catch-as-catch-can with the probabilities a hundred to one against success? It is not. Is singing a lost art? It is not. Let us get away from fad, fancy and formula and see the thing as it is. The problem is psychologic rather than physiologic. The fact that one may learn all that can be known about physiology and still know nothing whatever about voice training should awaken us to its uselessness.

17

Man is a mental entity. When I speak to a student *it is his mind that hears, not his body*. It is his mind that acts. It is his mind that originates and controls action. Therefore it is his mind that must be trained.

Action is not in the body. In fact, the body as matter has no sensation. Remove mind from the body and it does not 49feel. It is the mind that feels. If you believe that the body feels you must be prepared to explain where in the process of digestion and assimilation the beefsteak and potato you ate for dinner become conscious, because to feel they must be conscious. We know that the fluids and solids composing the body have no sensation when they are taken into the body, nor do they ever become sentient. Therefore the body of itself has no initiative, no action, no control. All of these are the functions of mind, hence the incongruity of attempting to solve a problem which is altogether psychological, which demands qualities of mind, habits of mind, mental concepts of a particular kind and quality, by a process of manipulation of the organ through which mind expresses itself, making the training of the mind a secondary matter; and then absurdly calling it scientific.

In every form of activity two things are involved: first, the idea: second, its expression. It must be apparent then, that the quality of the thing expressed will be governed by the quality of the idea. Or, to put it in another way: In the activity of art two things are involved—subject-matter and technic. The subject-matter, the substance of art, is mental. Technic is gaining such control of the medium that the subject-matter, or idea, may be fully and perfectly expressed. Ideas are the only substantial things in the universe, and that there is a difference in the quality of ideas need not be argued. Two men of the same avoirdupois may be walking side by side on the street, but one of them may be a genius and the other a hod carrier.

I have dwelt at some length on this because I wish to show where the training of a singer must begin, and that when we understand the real nature of the problem its solution becomes simple.

50

INDIRECT CONTROL

What is meant by indirect control? It means, in short, the automatic response of the mechanism to the idea. By way of illustration. If I should ask my pupil to make her vocal cords vibrate at the rate of 435 times per second she could not do it because she would have no mental concept of how it should sound: but if I strike the A above middle C and ask her to sing it her vocal cords respond automatically at that rate of vibration. It is the concept of pitch which forms the vocal instrument, gives it the exact amount of tension necessary to vibrate at the rate of the pitch desired, but the action is automatic, not the result of direct effort.

It may be said that in artistic singing everything is working automatically. There can be no such thing as artistic singing until everything involved is responding automatically to the mental demands of the singer.

Mention has been made of the automatic response of the vocal cords to the thought of pitch. That part of the mechanism which is so largely responsible for tone quality, the pharynx and mouth, must respond in the same way. This it will do unerringly if it is free from tension. But if the throat is full of rigidity, as is so often the condition, it cannot respond; consequently the quality is imperfect and the tone is throaty. The vocal cavity must vibrate in sympathy with the pitch in order to create pure resonance. It can do this only when it is free and is responding automatically to the concept of tone quality. To form the mouth and throat by direct effort and expect a good tone to result thereby, is an action not only certain of failure but exceedingly stupid.

VOICE TRAINING IS SIMPLE

There is a belief amounting to a solid conviction in the public 51mind that the training of the voice is so difficult that the probabilities of success are about one in ten. What is responsible for this? Doubtless the large number of failures. But this calls for another interrogation. What is the cause of these failures? Here is one. All students have done more or less singing before they go to a teacher. During that time they have, with scarcely an exception, formed bad habits. Now bad habits of voice production are almost invariably some form of throat interference, referred to as tension, rigidity, resistance, etc. Instances without number could be cited where students have been told to keep right on singing and eventually they would outgrow these habits. Such a thing never happened since time began. One may as well tell a drunkard to keep on drinking and eventually he will outgrow the habit. No. Something definite and specific must be done. The antidote for tension is relaxation. A muscle cannot respond while it is rigid, therefore the student must be taught how to get rid of tension.

TWO THINGS INVOLVED

There is nothing in voice training that is necessarily mysterious and inscrutable. On the contrary, if one will acquaint himself with its fundamental principles he will find that the truth about voice training, like all truth, is simple and easily understood, and when understood the element of uncertainty is eliminated. These principles are few in number, in fact they may all be brought under two general heads. The first is **KNOW WHAT YOU WANT**. The second is **HAVE THE CONDITIONS RIGHT**. The meaning of these statements can never be learned from a study of vocal physiology; nevertheless they contain all of the law and the prophets on this 52subject. Any musician may be a successful teacher of singing if he will master them. I use the word *musician*advisedly, because musical sense is of such vital importance that no amount of mechanical knowledge can take its place. To undertake the training of voices with only a mechanical knowledge of the subject is a handicap which no one can overcome.

It is universally true that the less one knows of the art of singing the more he concerns himself with the mechanism; and it is also true that the more one is filled with the spirit of song the less he concerns himself with the construction of the vocal instrument. People with little or no musicianship have been known to wrangle ceaselessly on whether or not the thyroid cartilage should tip forward on high tones. It is such crude mechanics masquerading under the name of science that has brought voice training into general disrepute. The voice teacher is primarily concerned with learning to play upon the vocal instrument rather than upon its mechanical construction, two things which some find difficulty in separating.

KNOW WHAT YOU WANT

This means much. In voice production it means the perfect tone concept. It means far more than knowing what one likes. What one likes and what he ought to like are usually quite different things. What one likes is the measure of his taste at that particular time and may or may not be an argument in its favor. I have never seen a beginner whose taste was perfectly formed, but the great majority of them know what they like, and because they like a certain kind of tone, or a certain way of singing, they take it for granted that it is right until they are shown something better. This error is by no means confined to beginners.

53If your pupil does not produce good tone one of two things is responsible for it. Either he does not know a good tone or else the conditions are not right. In the beginning it is usually both. Your pupil must create his tone mentally before he sings it. He must create its quality no less than its pitch. In other words *he must hear his tone before he sings it and then sing what he hears.* Until he can do this his voice will have no character. His voice will be as indefinite as his tone concept, and it will not improve until his concept, which is his taste, improves. Inasmuch as everything exists first as idea, it follows that everything which is included in the rightly produced voice and in interpretation are first matters of concept. The singer uses a certain tone quality because he mentally conceives that quality to be right. He delivers a word or phrase in a certain way because that is his concept of it.

A word at this point on imitation. One faculty of a musical mind is that of recording mentally what it hears and of producing it mentally whenever desired. Most people possess this in some degree, and some people in a marked degree. Almost any one can hear mentally the tone of a cornet, violin, or any instrument with which he is acquainted. In the same way the vocal student must hear mentally the pure singing tone before he can sing it. It is the business of the teacher to assist him in forming a perfect tone concept, and if he can do this by example, as well as by precept, he has a distinct advantage over the one who cannot.

Arguments against imitation are not uncommon, and yet the teachers who offer them will advise their students to hear the great singers as often as possible. Such incongruities do not inspire confidence.

On this human plane most things are learned by imitation. What language would the child speak if it were never allowed 54to hear spoken language? It would never be anything but

"An infant crying in the night.
And with no language but a cry."

There are but few original thinkers on earth at any one time. The rest are imitators and none too perfect at that. We are imitators in everything from religion to breakfast foods. Few of us ever have an original idea. We trail along from fifty to a hundred years behind those we are trying to imitate.

When there is little else but imitation going on in the world why deny it to vocal students? The argument against imitation can come from but two classes of people—those who cannot produce a good tone and those who are more interested in how the tone is made than in the tone itself.

The following are the qualities the teacher undertakes to develop in the student in preparing him for artistic singing. They are fundamental and must be a part of the singer's equipment no matter what method is employed. They are what all musicians expect to hear in the trained singer. They all exist first as concepts.

An even scale from top to bottom of the voice.

19

Every tone full of strength and character.

A sympathetic quality.

Ample power.

A clear, telling resonance in every tone.

A pure legato and sostenuto.

Perfect freedom in production throughout the compass.

A perfect swell, that is, the ability to go from pianissimo to full voice and return, on any tone in the compass, without a break, and without sacrificing the tone quality.

The ability to pronounce distinctly and with ease to the top of the compass.

Equal freedom in the delivery of vowels and consonants.

55Sufficient flexibility to meet all technical demands.

An ear sensitive to the finest shades of intonation.

An artistic concept or interpretive sense of the highest possible order.

The process of acquiring these things is not accretion but *unfoldment*. It is the unfoldment of ideas or concepts. The growth of ideas is similar to that of plants and flowers. The growth of expression follows the growth of the idea, it never precedes it. From the formation of the first vowel to the perfect interpretation of a song the teacher is dealing with mental concepts.

At the Gobelin Tapestry works near Paris I was told that the weavers of those wonderful tapestries use twenty-four shades of each color, and that their color sense becomes so acute that they readily recognize all of the different shades. Now there are about as many shades of each vowel, and the mental picture of the vowel must be so definite, the mental ear so sensitive, that it will detect the slightest variation from the perfect form. Direct control could never accomplish this. Only the automatic response of the mechanism to the perfect vowel concept can result in a perfect vowel.

All of those qualities and elements mentioned above as constituting the artist come under the heading **KNOW WHAT YOU WANT**.

The second step **HAVE THE CONDITIONS RIGHT** means, in short, to free the mechanism of all interference and properly manage the breath. This getting rid of interference could be talked about indefinitely without wasting time. It is far more important than most people suspect. Few voices are entirely free from it, and when it is present in a marked degree it is an effectual bar to progress. So long as it is present in the slightest degree it affects the tone quality. Most students think they are through with it long before they are.

56This interference, which is referred to as tension, rigidity, throatiness, etc., is in the nature of resistance to the free emission of tone. It is not always confined to the vocal cords, but usually extends to the walls of the pharynx and the body of the tongue. The vocal cavities, the pharynx and mouth, exert such a marked influence on tone quality that the least degree of rigidity produces an effect that is instantly noticeable to the trained ear. These parts of the vocal mechanism which are so largely responsible not only for perfect vowels, but for perfect tone quality as well, must at all times be so free from tension that they can respond instantly to the tone concept. If they fail to respond the tone will be imperfect, and these imperfections are all classed under the general head "throaty." Throaty tone means that there is resistance somewhere, and the conditions will never be right until the last vestige of it is destroyed. The difficulty in voice placing which so many have, lies in trying to produce the upper tones without first getting rid of resistance. This condition is responsible for a number of shop-worn statements, such as "bring the tone forward," "place the tone in the head," "direct the tone into the head," etc. I recall a writer who says that the column of breath must be directed against the hard palate toward the front of the mouth in order to get a resonant tone. Consider this a moment. When the breath is properly vocalized its power is completely destroyed. Any one may test this by vocalizing in an atmosphere cold enough to condense the moisture in his breath. If he is vocalizing perfectly, he will observe that the breath moves lazily out of the mouth and curls upward not more than an inch from the face. The idea that this breath, which has not a particle of force after leaving the vocal cords, can be directed against the hard palate with an impact sufficient to affect tone quality is the limit of absurdity. If the writer had spoken of directing the sound waves to the front of the mouth 57there would have been an element of reasonableness in it, for sound waves can be reflected as well as light waves; but breath and sound are quite different things.

What does the teacher mean when he tells the pupil to place the tone in the head? He doubtless means that the student shall call into use the upper resonator. If one holds a vibrating tuning-fork before a resonating tube, does he direct the vibrations into that resonating cavity? No. Neither is it necessary to try to drive the voice into the cavities of the head. Such instructions are of doubtful value. They are almost sure to result in a hard unsympathetic tone. They increase rather than diminish the resistance. The only possible way to place the tone in the head is to let it go there. This will always occur when the resistance is destroyed and the channel is free.

In numerous instances the resistance in the vocal cords is so great that it is impossible to sing softly, or with half voice. It requires so much breath pressure to start the vibration, that is, to overcome the resistance, that when it does start it is with full voice. In a majority of male voices the upper tone must be taken either with full chest voice or with falsetto. There is no *mezza voce*. This condition is abnormal and is responsible for the "red in the face" brand of voice production so often heard.

Of this we may be sure, that no one can sing a good full tone unless he can sing a good *mezza voce*. When the mechanism is sufficiently free from resistance that a good pianissimo can be sung then the conditions are right to begin to build toward a *forte*.

Further, when the mechanism is entirely free from resistance there is no conscious effort required to produce tone. The singer has the feeling of letting himself sing rather than of making himself sing.

The engineer of a great pumping station once told me that 58his mammoth Corliss engine was so perfectly balanced that he could run it with ten pounds of steam. When the voice is free, and resting on the breath as it were, it seems to sing itself.

An illustration of the opposite condition, of extreme resistance was once told me by the president of a great street railway system that was operated by a cable. He said it required eighty-five per cent of the power generated to start the machinery, that is, to overcome the resistance, leaving but fifteen per cent for operating cars. It is not at all uncommon to hear singers who are so filled with resistance that it requires all of their available energy to make the vocal instrument produce tone. Such singers soon find themselves exhausted and the voice tired and husky. It is this type of voice production rather than climatic conditions, that causes so much chronic laryngitis among singers. I have seen the truth of this statement verified in the complete and permanent disappearance of many cases of laryngitis through learning to produce the voice correctly.

The second step in securing right conditions is the proper management of the breath.

BREATH CONTROL

An extremist always lacks the sense of proportion. He allows a single idea to fill his mental horizon. He is fanciful, and when an idea comes to him he turns his high power imagination upon it, and it immediately becomes overwhelming in magnitude and importance. Thereafter all things in his universe revolve around it.

The field of voice teaching is well stocked with extremists. Everything involved in voice production and many things that are not, have been taken up one at a time and made the basis of a method.

59One builds his reputation on a peculiar way of getting the tone into the frontal sinuses by way of the infundibulum canal, and makes all other things secondary.

Another has discovered a startling effect which a certain action of the arytenoid cartilages has on registers, and sees a perfect voice as the result.

Another has discovered that a particular movement of the thyroid cartilage is the only proper way to tense the vocal cords and when every one learns to do this all bad voices will disappear.

Another has discovered something in breath control so revolutionary in its nature that it alone will solve all vocal problems.

Perhaps if all of these discoveries could be combined they might produce something of value; but who will undertake it? Not the extremists themselves, for they are barren of the synthetic idea, and their sense of proportion is rudimentary. They would be scientists were it not for their abnormal imaginations. The scientist takes the voice apart and examines it in detail, but the voice teacher must put all parts of it together and mold it into a perfect whole. The process is synthetic rather than analytic, and undue emphasis on any one element destroys the necessary balance.

The immediate danger of laying undue emphasis on any one idea in voice training lies in its tendency toward the mechanical and away from the spontaneous, automatic response so vitally necessary. Here the extremists commit a fatal error. To make breath management the all-in-all of singing invariably leads to direct control, and soon the student has become so conscious of the mechanism of breathing that his mind is never off of it while singing; he finds himself becoming rigid trying to prevent his breath from escaping, and the more rigid he becomes the less control he has. A 60large number of examples of this kind of breath management have come under my observation. They all show the evil results of over working an idea.

But the followers of "the-breath-is-the-whole-thing" idea say "You can't sing without breath control." Solomon never said a truer thing, but the plan just mentioned is the worst possible way to secure it.

21

Every one should know that not a single one of the processes of voice production is right until it is working automatically, and automatic action is the result of indirect, never of direct control.

The profession has become pretty thoroughly imbued with the idea that deep breathing, known as abdominal, or diaphragmatic is the best for purposes of singing. But how deep? The answer is, the deeper the better. Here again it is easy to overstep the bounds. I have in mind numerous instances where the singer, under the impression that he was practicing deep breathing tried to control the breath with the lower abdominal muscles, but no matter how great the effort made there was little tonal response, for the reason that the pressure exerted was not against the lungs but against the contents of the abdomen. The diaphragm is the point of control. The lungs lie above it, not below it. To concentrate the thought on the lower abdominal muscles means to lose control of the diaphragm, the most important thing involved in breath management.

The process of breathing is simple. The lungs are enclosed in an air tight box of which the diaphragm is the bottom. It rests under the lungs like an inverted saucer. In the act of contracting it flattens toward a plane and in so doing it moves downward and forward, away from the lungs. The ribs move outward, forward and upward. The lungs which occupy this box like a half compressed sponge follow the receding walls, 61and a vacuum is created which air rushes in to fill. In exhalation the action is reversed. The ribs press against the lungs and the diaphragm slowly returns to its original position and the breath is forced out like squeezing water out of a sponge.

The one important thing in breath management is the diaphragm. If the student has the right action of the diaphragm he will have no further trouble with breath control. In my Systematic Voice Training will be found a list of exercises which thoroughly cover the subject of breath control and if properly used will correct all errors. Let this be understood, that there is nothing in correct breathing that should make one tired. On the contrary the practice of breathing should leave one refreshed. Above all, the student should never make himself rigid when trying to control the flow of breath. This is not only of no advantage, but will effectually defeat the end for which he is striving.

REGISTERS

In securing right conditions the teacher is often confronted with the problem of registers. The literature on this subject is voluminous and varied. Opinions are offered without stint and the number of registers which have been discovered in the human voice ranges from none to an indefinite number. How one scientist can see two, and another one five registers in the same voice might be difficult to explain were it not a well known fact that some people are better at "seeing things" than others.

But here again the teacher soon learns that laboratory work is of little value. His view point is so different from that of the physicist that they can hardly be said to be working at the 62same problem. The physicist tries to discover the action of the mechanism, in other words, how the tone is made. The voice teacher is concerned primarily with how it sounds. One is looking at the voice, the other is listening to it, which things, be it known, are essentially and fundamentally different; so different that their relationship is scarcely traceable. The ability to train the voice comes through working with voices where the musical sense, rather than the scientific sense, is the guide. It is a specific knowledge which can be gained in no other way. It begins when one takes an untrained voice and attempts to make it produce a musical tone.

The problem of registers is, in short, how to make an even scale out of an uneven one. It must be solved in the studio. Anatomical knowledge is of no avail. The teacher who has learned how to produce an even scale possesses knowledge which is of more value to the student than all of the books ever written on vocal mechanism.

The depressions in the voice known as "changes of register" result from tension. With one adjustment of the vocal cords the singer can, by adding tension, make a series of four or five tones, then by a change of adjustment he can produce another similar series, and so on to the top of his compass. These changes occur when there is such an accumulation of tension that no more can be added to that adjustment without discomfort. The solution of this problem lies in gaining such freedom from tension in the vocal instrument that it automatically readjusts itself for each tone. The tension is then evenly distributed throughout the scale and the sudden changes disappear. This is precisely what happens when the singer has learned to produce an even scale throughout his compass; his voice production is not right until he can do this.

The statement is frequently made in public print that there are no registers in the trained voice. This order of wisdom is 63equally scintillating with that profound intellectual effort which avers that a bald headed man has no hair on the top of his head, or that hot weather is due to a rise in the temperature. These statements may be heavy-laden with truth, but to the voice teacher they are irrelevant. His work is at least seven-eighths with untrained voices. By the time he has worked out an even scale with all of the other problems that go hand in hand with it, for a great deal of the art of singing will naturally accompany it, a large majority of his pupils are ready to move on. Only a small per cent prepare for a musical career. Most of his work is with voices that still need to be perfected. It is for voices of this kind that the teacher lives. It is for such voices that vocal methods are evolved and books written.

A lighthearted, easy going assurance is not sufficient alone to compass the problems that present themselves in the studio. If the teacher is conscientious there will be times when he will feel deeply the need of something more than human wisdom. The work in the studio has more to do with the future than with the immediate present. The singing lesson is a small part of what the student carries with him. The atmosphere of the studio, which is the real personality of the teacher, his ideals, aims, the depth of his sincerity, in short, his concept of the meaning of life, goes with the student and will be remembered when the lesson is forgotten.

64

V
THE NATURE AND MEANING OF ART

One function, then, of art is to feed and mature the imagination and the spirit, and thereby enhance and invigorate the whole of human life.

Ancient Art and Ritual. Jane Ellen Harrison.

A large percentage of the population of the civilized world has more or less to do with what is called art. In its various forms art touches in some degree practically the entire human race. Its various activities have developed great industries, and for the entertainment it affords fabulous sums of money are spent.

What is this thing called art which takes such a hold upon the human race? If it has no social or economic value then a vast amount of time and money are wasted each year in its study and practice. A brief inquiry into the nature and meaning of art may well be associated with a discussion of the art of singing.

Art as a whole comes under the head of Aesthetics, which may be defined as the philosophy of taste, the science of the beautiful.

It will doubtless be admitted without argument that ever since the dawn of consciousness the visible world has produced sense impressions differing from each other—some pleasant, some unpleasant. From these different sense impressions there gradually evolved what is known as beauty and ugliness. An attempt to discover the principles underlying beauty and ugliness resulted in Aesthetics, the founder of which was Baumgarten (1714-1762).

It will be interesting to hear what he and the later aestheticians have to say about art. Most of them connect it in 65some way with that which is beautiful, that is, pleasing, but they do not all agree in their definition of beauty.

Baumgarten defined beauty as the perfect, the absolute, recognized through the senses. He held that the highest embodiment of beauty is seen by us in nature, therefore the highest aim of art is to copy nature.

Winkelmann (1717-1768) held the law and aim of art to be beauty independent of goodness. Hutcheson (1694-1747) was of essentially the same opinion.

According to Kant (1724-1804) beauty is that which pleases without the reasoning process.

Schiller (1758-1805) held that the aim of art is beauty, the source of which is pleasure without practical advantage.

These definitions do not wholly satisfy. They do not accord to art the dignified position it should hold in social development. But there are others who have a clearer vision. Fichte (1762-1814) said that beauty exists not in the visible world but in the beautiful soul, and that art is the manifestation of this beautiful soul, and that its aim is the education of the whole man.

In this we begin to see the real nature and activity of art. There are other aestheticians who define art in much the same way.

Shaftesbury (1670-1713) said that beauty is recognized by the mind only. God is fundamental beauty.

Hegel (1770-1831) said: "Art is God manifesting himself in the form of beauty. Beauty is the idea shining through matter. Art is a means of bringing to consciousness and expressing the deepest problems of humanity and the highest truths." According to Hegel beauty and truth are one and the same thing.

Thus we see that the great thinkers of the world make art of supreme importance in the perfecting of the human race. 66They all agree that art is not in material objects, but is a condition and activity of spirit. They agree in the main that beauty and truth emanate from the same source. Said Keats:

"Beauty is truth and truth beauty,
That is all ye know on earth and all ye need know."

23

Said Schelling: "Beauty is the perception of the Infinite in the finite."

But perhaps the highest concept of art is from the great artist Whistler. He said: "Art is an expression of eternal absolute truth, and starting from the Infinite it cannot progress, **IT IS**."

Art in some form and in some degree finds a response in every one. Why? Because every one consciously or unconsciously is looking toward and striving for perfection. This is the law of being. Every one is seeking to improve his condition, and this means that in some degree every one is an idealist. Ever since time began idealism has been at work, and to it we owe every improved condition—social, political and religious.

Hegel believed that the aim of art is to portray nature in perfect form, not with the imperfections seen around us; and Herbert Spencer defined art as the attempt to realize the ideal in the present. The artist tries to make his picture more perfect than what he sees around him. The poet, the sculptor, the musician, the craftsman, the mechanic, are all striving for a more perfect expression, because perfection is the fundamental, eternal law of being.

Wagner said: "The world will be redeemed through art," and if Whistler's definition be accepted he is not far from the truth.

The important thing to remember is that art is not a mere pastime, but a great world force operating to lift mortals out of mortality. It is the striving of the finite to reach the Infinite.

67In human history art, no less than languages, has conformed to the theory of evolution. Language in the beginning was monosyllabic. Far back in the early dawn of the race, before the development of the community spirit, when feelings, emotions, ideas, were simple and few the medium of expression was simple, and it grew with the demand for a larger expression.

This same process of evolution is seen in the growth of each individual. The child, seeing grimalkin stalk stealthily into the room, points the finger and says "cat." This is the complete expression of itself on that subject. It is the sum total of its knowledge of zoology at that particular moment; and a long process of development must follow before it will refer to the same animal as a "Felis Domestica."

In a similar way musical expression keeps step with musical ideas. In the beginning musical ideas were short, simple, fragmentary, monosyllabic, mere germs of melody (adherents of the germ theory will make a note of this). The Arab with his rudimentary fiddle will repeat this fragment of melody by the hour, while a company of his unlaundered brethren dance, until exhausted, in dust to their ankles, with the temperature near the boiling point. This musical monosyllable is ample to satisfy his artistic craving. In other words it is the complete musical expression of himself.

The following is a complete program of dance music for the aborigines of Australia. The repetition of this figure may continue for hours. If it were inflicted on a metropolitan audience it would result in justifiable homicide, but to the Australian it furnishes just the emotional stimulus he desires.

68 This one from Tongtoboo, played Allegro, would set the heels of any company, ancient or modern, in motion.

These people may be said to be in the rhythmic stage of music, that is, a stage of development in which a rhythmic movement which serves to incite the dance furnishes complete artistic satisfaction.

As it is a long distance from the monosyllabic expression of the child to the point where he can think consecutively in polysyllabic dissertation, so it is an equally long distance from the inarticulate musical utterances of the barbarous tribes to the endless melodies of Wagner, which begin at 8 P. M. and continue until 12.15 A. M. without repetition.

Following the course of music from the beginning we shall see that it has kept pace with civilization. As the race has grown mentally it has expressed itself in a larger and more perfect way in its literature, its painting and music. Physically the race has not grown perceptibly in the last five thousand years, but mentally its growth can scarcely be measured. If we follow each nation through the past thousand years we shall see that its art product has not only kept pace with its development, but that in its art we may see all of its racial characteristics, those habits of mind which are peculiarly its own. A nation left to itself will develop a certain trend of thought which will differentiate it from all other nations. A trend of thought which will affect its art, literature, politics, religion, and in course of time will produce marked physical characteristics. This is noticeable in all nations which have lived long unto themselves.

But modern methods of communication are destroying this. As nations are brought into closer contact with each other they 69begin to lose their peculiarities. The truth of this statement may be seen in the fact that in the past fifty years composers all over the world have been affected by the modern German school of composition. Not one has escaped. While a nation lived unto itself it could preserve its national life in its art, but more and more the life of each nation is becoming a composite of the life of all nations. The musical output of the world shows this unmistakably.

What will be the music of the future? We know the music of yesterday and today, but the music of the future can be foretold only by the prophet whose vision is clear enough to see unmistakably what the trend of civilization will be during the coming years. There are mighty forces operating in the world today. If they succeed in bringing humanity to a saner, more normal state of mind, to a clearer realization of what is worth while and what is worthless, then all art will become purer and more wholesome, more helpful and necessary, and music speaking a language common to all will be supreme among the arts.

70

VI
SINGING AS AN ART

No artist can be graceful, imaginative, or original, unless he be truthful.

Ruskin. *Modern Painters.*

"Art is a transfer of feeling" said Tolstoy. While this applies to art in general it has a particular application to the art of singing. The material of the singer's art is feeling. By means of the imagination he evokes within himself feelings he has experienced and through the medium of his voice he transfers these feelings to others. By his ability to reconstruct moods, feelings and emotions within himself and express them through his voice, the singer sways multitudes, plays upon them, carries them whithersoever he will from the depths of sorrow to the heights of exaltation. His direct and constant aim is to make his hearers *feel*, and feel deeply. As a medium for the transfer of feeling the human voice far transcends all others. Since the beginning of the human race the voice has been the means by which it has most completely revealed itself, but the art is not in the voice, but in the feeling transferred. It is the same whether the medium be the voice, painting, sculpture, poetry or a musical instrument. We speak of a painting as being a great work of art, but the art is not in the painting, the art is the feeling of beauty which the painting awakes in the observer. When we listen to an orchestra the music is what we feel. Said Walt Whitman: "Music is what awakes within us when we are reminded by the instruments."

Nothing exists separate from cognition. Real art therefore consists of pure feeling rather than of material objects. *If the singer succeeds in transferring his feelings to others he is an artist,* this regardless of whether his voice is great or small. 71Voice alone does not constitute an artist. One must have something to give. Schumann said: "The reason the nightingale sings love songs and the lap dog barks is because the soul of the nightingale is filled with love and that of the lap dog with bark." It will be apparent therefore, that the study of the art of singing should devote itself to developing in the singer the best elements of his nature—all that is good, pure and elevating. We have no right to transfer to others any feeling that is impure or unwholesome. The technic of an art is of small moment compared with its subject matter. *An unworthy poem cannot be purified by setting it to music no matter how beautiful the music may be.*

THE PRINCIPLES OF INTERPRETATION

I fancy there is nothing more intangible to most people than the term *"phrasing."* I have asked a great many students to give me the principles of phrasing, but as yet I have seen none who could do it, and yet all singers, from the youngest to the oldest must make some use of these principles every time they sing. Now a thing in such general use should be, and is, subject to analysis.

All of the rules of phrasing, like the rules of composition, grow out of what sounds well. Beauty and ugliness are matters of mental correspondence. In music a thing to be beautiful must satisfy a mental demand, and this demand is one's *taste.* The sense of fitness must obtain. When the singer interprets a song the demand of the listener is that he shall do well what he undertakes to do: that he shall portray whatever phase of life the song contains, accurately, definitely, that he shall have a *definite intent and purpose,* that he shall be in the mood of the song. The singer must not portray one mood with his 72face, another with his voice, while the poem suggests still a third. He must avoid incongruity. All things must work together. There must be therefore, the evidence of intelligent design in every word and phrase.

The song is a unit and each phrase contains a definite idea, therefore it must not be detached or fragmentary, but must have the element of continuity and each and every part must be made to contribute to the central idea.

The element of insecurity must not be allowed to enter. If it does, the listener feels that the singer is not sure of himself, that he cannot do what he set out to do: therefore he is a failure.

Another demand is that the singer shall be intelligent. A poem does not lose its meaning or its strength by being associated with music, and to this end the singer must deliver the text with the same understanding and appreciation of its meaning as would a public reader.

25

Now from the above we infer certain principles. The demand for continuity means that the singer must have a pure *legato*. That is, he must be able to connect words smoothly, to pass from one word to another without interrupting the tone, that the tone may be continuous throughout each phrase.

The feeling of security lies in what is known as *sostenuto*, the ability to sustain the tone throughout the phrase with no sense of diminishing power. It means in short the organ time.

From the demand for design in each word and phrase comes *contrast*. This may be made in the power of the tone by means of cres. dim. sfz. It may be made in the tempo by means of the retard, accelerando, the hold, etc. It may also be made in the quality of the tone by using the various shades from bright to somber.

The basis of phrasing then, may be found in legato, sostenuto and contrast. All of the other things involved in 73interpretation cannot make a good performance if these fundamental principles be lacking. A more complete outline of interpretation follows:

AN OUTLINE OF INTERPRETATION

REA
DING
Pitches
Note
Lengths
Rhythm

DIC
TION
Enunciation
Vow
els
Consonants
Pronunciati
on
Accent
Emphasis

VOI
CE
Even Scale
Quality
Freedom
Breath
Control

TEC
HNIC
Attack
Flexibility
Execution

PHR
ASING
Legato
Sostenuto
Contrast
Pow
er
Tempo
Color
Proportion

MO
OD
Emotional
Concept
Facial
Expression
Stage
Presence

26

Most of the things mentioned in this outline of interpretation have been discussed elsewhere, but the subject of diction requires further explanation.
74

DICTION

The mechanism of speech might be discussed at any length, but to reduce it to its simplest form it consists of the sound producing instrument,—the vocal cords, the organs of enunciation—lips, tongue, teeth and soft palate, and the channel leading to the outer air. When the vocal cords are producing pitch and the channel is free the result is a vowel. If an obstruction is thrown into the channel the result is a consonant. Vowels and consonants, then, constitute the elements of speech. The vowels are the emotional elements and the consonants are the intellectual elements. By means of vowel sounds alone emotions may be awakened, but when definite ideas are expressed, words which are a combination of vowels and consonants must be used. It is nothing short of amazing that with this simple mechanism, by using the various combinations of open and obstructed channel in connection with pitch, the entire English language or any other language for that matter can be produced.

Vowels are produced with an open channel from the vocal cords to the outer air. Consonants are produced with partial or complete closing of the channel by interference of the lips, tongue, teeth and soft palate.

If language consisted entirely of vowels learning to sing would be much simpler than it is. It is the consonants that cause trouble. It is not uncommon to find students who can vocalize with comparative ease, but the moment they attempt to sing words the mechanism becomes rigid. The tendency toward rigidity is much greater in enunciating consonants than it is in enunciating vowels, and yet they should be equally easy. Here is where the student finds his greatest difficulty in mastering English diction.

The most frequent criticism of American singers is their 75deficiency in diction. Whether it please us or no, it must be admitted that on the whole the criticism is not without foundation.

The importance of effective speech is much underestimated by students of singing, and yet it requires but a moment's consideration to see that the impression created by speech is the result of forceful diction no less than of subject matter. Words mean the same thing whether spoken or sung, and the singer no less than the speaker should deliver them with a full understanding of their meaning.

The proposition confronting the singer is a difficult one. When he attempts the dramatic he finds that it destroys his legato. He loses the sustained quality of the organ tone, which is the true singing tone, and *bel canto* is out of the question.

This is what is urged against the operas of Wagner and practically everything of the German school since his day. The dramatic element is so intense and the demand so strenuous that singers find it almost, if not quite impossible, to keep the singing tone and reach the dramatic heights required. They soon find themselves shouting in a way that not only destroys the singing tone but also the organ that produces it. The truth of this cannot be gainsaid. There is a considerable amount of vocal wreckage strewn along the way, the result of wrestling with Wagnerian recitative. Wagnerian singers are, as a rule, vocally shorter lived than those that confine themselves to French and Italian opera.

But it will be argued by some that these people have not learned how to sing, that if they had a perfect vocal method they could sing Wagner as easily as Massenet. That they have not learned to sing Wagner is evident, and this brings us to the question—Shall the singer adjust himself to the composer or the composer to the singer? A discussion of this would probably lead nowhere, but I submit the observation, that 76many modern composers show a disregard for the possibilities and limitations of the human voice that amounts to stupidity. Because a composer can write great symphonies the public is inclined to think that everything he writes is great. Let it be understood once for all that bad voice writing is bad whether it is done by a symphonic writer or a popular songwriter. In the present stage of human development there are certain things the voice can do and other things it cannot do, and these things can be known only by those who understand the voice, and are accustomed to working with it. To ignore them completely when writing for voices is no evidence of genius. Composers seem to forget that the singer must create the pitch of his instrument as well as its quality at the moment he uses it. They also forget that his most important aid in this is the feeling of tonality. When this is destroyed and the singer is forced to measure intervals abstractedly he is called upon to do something immeasurably more difficult than anything that is asked of the instrumentalist. Many modern composers have lost their heads and run amuck on the modern idiom, and their writing for voices is so complex that it would require a greater musician to sing their music than it did to write it.

But to return, I do not say that it is impossible to apply the principles of *bel canto* to Wagner's dramatic style of utterance. On the contrary I believe it is possible to gain such a mastery of voice production and enunciation that the Wagnerian roles may be sung, not shouted, and still not be lacking in dramatic intensity, but it requires a more careful study of diction and its relation to voice production than most singers are willing to make.

A majority of singers never succeed in establishing the right relation between the vocal organ and the organs of enunciation. Years of experience have verified this beyond peradventure.

It is a very common thing for singers to vocalize for an indefinite 77period with no ill effect, but become hoarse with ten minutes of singing. The reason is apparent. They have learned how to produce vowels with a free throat but not consonants. The moment they attempt to form a consonant, tension appears, not only in those parts of the mechanism which form the consonant, but in the vocal organ as well. Under such treatment the voice soon begins to show wear, and this is exactly what happens to those singers who find it difficult to sing the Wagner operas.

The solution of this problem lies in the proper study of diction. The intellectual elements of speech consonants are formed almost entirely in the front of the mouth with various combinations of lips, tongue and teeth. Three things are necessary to their complete mastery.

First,—consonants must be produced without tension. It will be well to remember in this connection that consonants are not to be sung. They are points of interference and must be distinct but short. The principle of freedom applies to consonants no less than to vowels.

Second,—consonants must not be allowed to interrupt the continuity of the pitch produced by the vocal cords. This is necessary to preserve legato. Some consonants close the channel completely, others only partially. It is a great achievement to be able to sing all consonant combinations and still preserve a legato.

Third,—consonants must in no way interfere with the freedom of the vocal organ. If the student attempts to sing the consonants, that is, to prolong them he is sure to make his throat rigid and the pure singing tone at once disappears. He must therefore learn dramatic utterance without throwing the weight of it on the throat. To do this he must begin with a consonant which offers the least resistance and practice it until the three points mentioned have been mastered. The 78one which will give the least trouble is l. At the pitch G sing ah-lah-lah-lah-lah, until it can be done with relaxed tongue, with perfect continuity of tone, and with perfect freedom in the vocal instrument. In the same way practice n, d, v, th, m, and the sub vocals, b, d, g. Always begin with a vowel.

If the singer has the patience to work the problem out in this way he can apply the principles of *bel canto* to dramatic singing. The road to this achievement is long, longer than most people suspect, but if one is industrious and persevering it may be accomplished.

But there remains yet to be mentioned the most important element of artistic singing. To the pure tone and perfect diction must be added the imagination. The *imagination* is the image making power of the mind, the power to create or reproduce ideally that which has been previously perceived: the power to call up mental images. By means of the imagination we take the materials of experience and mold them into idealized forms. The aim of creative art is to idealize, that is, to portray nature and experience in perfect forms not with the imperfections of visible nature. "In this" says Hegel, "art is superior to nature."

The activity of the imagination is directly responsible for that most essential thing—emotional tone. Taking intelligence for granted, the imagination is the most important factor involved in interpretation. If the imagination be quick and responsive it will carry the singer away from himself and temporarily he will live the song.

Every song has an atmosphere, a metaphysical something which differentiates it from every other song. The singer must discover it and find the mood which will perfectly express it. If his imagination constructs the image, creates the picture, recalls the feeling, the emotion, the result will be artistic singing. The song is that which comes from the soul 79of the singer. It is not on the printed page. If I study a Schubert song until I have mastered it, I have done nothing to Schubert. It is I who have grown. Through the activity of the imagination, guided by the intelligence, I have built up in my consciousness as nearly as possible what I conceive to have been Schubert's feeling when he wrote the song, but the work has all been done on myself.

A chapter might be written on the artistic personality. It reveals itself in light, shade, nuance, inflection, accent, color, always with a perfect sense of proportion, harmony and unity, and free from all that is earthy. It is the expression of individuality. It cannot be imitated. If you ask me for its source I repeat again Whistler's immortal saying: "Art is an expression of eternal, absolute truth, and starting from the Infinite it cannot progress,**IT IS.**"

80

VII

THE CONSTRUCTION OF A SONG.

Has he put the emphasis on his work in the place where it is most important? Has he so completely expressed himself that the onlooker cannot fail to find his meaning?

Appreciation of Art. Loveridge.

When you listen to a song and at its close say, "That is beautiful," do you ever stop and try to discover why it is beautiful? The quest may lead you far into the field of Aesthetics, and unless you are accustomed to psychological processes you may find yourself in a maze from which escape is difficult. Let us remember that in studying the construction of a song we are dealing with states of mind. A song is the product of a certain mood and its direct aim is to awaken a similar mood in others.

It is a well established fact that sound is the most common and the most effective way of expressing and communicating the emotions, not only for man but for the lower animals as well. This method of communication doubtless began far back in the history of the race and was used to express bodily pain or pleasure.

The lower animals convey their feelings to each other by sounds, not by words, and these sounds awaken in others the same feeling as that which produced them.

We see, then, that emotion may be expressed by sound and be awakened by sound, and this obtains among human beings no less than among the lower animals. In the long process of ages sound qualities have become indissolubly associated with emotional states, and have become the most exciting, the most powerful sense stimulus in producing emotional reactions. The cry of one human being in pain will excite 81painful emotions in another. An exclamation of joy will excite a similar emotion in others, and so on through the whole range of human emotions.

Herbert Spencer holds that the beginning of music may be traced back to the cry of animals, which evidently has an emotional origin and purpose. It is a far cry from the beginning of music as described by Spencer to the modern art song, but from that time to this the principle has remained the same. The emotional range of the lower animals is small, doubtless limited to the expression of bodily conditions, but the human race through long ages of growth has developed an almost unlimited emotional range, hence the vehicle for its expression has of necessity increased in complexity.

To meet this demand music as a science has evolved a tone system. That is, from the infinite number of tones it has selected something over a hundred having definite mathematical relationships, fixed vibrational ratios. The art of music takes this system of tones and by means of combinations, progressions and movements which constitute what is called musical composition, it undertakes to excite a wide variety of emotions.

The aim and office of music is to create moods. It does not arrive at definite expression. There is no musical progression which is universally understood as an invitation to one's neighbor to pass the bread. The pianist cannot by any particular tone combination make his audience understand that his left shoe pinches, but he can make them smile or look serious. He can fill them with courage or bring them to tears without saying a word. In listening to the Bach *B Minor Mass* one can tell the *Sanctus* from the *Gloria in Excelsis* without knowing a word of Latin. The music conveys the mood unmistakably.

A song is a union of music and poetry, a wedding if you please and as in all matrimonial alliances the two contracting parties should be in harmony. The poem creates a mood not alone by 82what it expresses directly but by what it implies, what it suggests. Its office is to stimulate the imagination rather than to inform by direct statement of facts. The office of music is to strengthen, accentuate, and supplement the mood of the poem, to translate the poem into music. The best song then, will be one in which both words and music most perfectly create the same mood.

Arnold Bennett's definition of literature applies equally well to the song. He says: "That evening when you went for a walk with your faithful friend, the friend from whom you hid nothing—or almost nothing—you were, in truth, somewhat inclined to hide from him the particular matter which monopolized your mind that evening, but somehow you contrived to get on to it, drawn by an overpowering fascination. And as your faithful friend was sympathetic and discreet, and flattered you by a respectful curiosity, you proceeded further and further into the said matter, growing more and more confidential, until at last you cried out in a terrific whisper: 'My boy she is simply miraculous:' At that moment you were in the domain of literature." Now when such impassioned, spontaneous utterance is brought under the operation of musical law we have a perfect song. The composer furnished the words and music, but the thing which makes it a song comes from the singer, from the earnestness and conviction with which he delivers the message.

Songs are divided into two general classes: those expressing the relationships of human beings, such as love, joy, sorrow, chivalry, patriotism, etc., and those expressing the relationship of man to his creator; veneration, devotion, praise, etc. The two great sources of inspiration to song writers have always been love and religion.

What are the principles of song construction? They are all comprised in the law of fitness. The composer must do what [83]he sets out to do. The materials with which he has to work are rhythm, melody and harmony. The most important thing in a song is the melody. This determines to a very great extent the health and longevity of the song. Most of the songs that have passed the century mark and still live do so by reason of their melody. There must be a sense of fitness between the poem and the melody. A poem which expresses a simple sentiment requires a simple melody. A simple story should be told simply. If the poem is sad, joyous, or tragic the melody must correspond. Otherwise the family discords begin at once. Poetry cannot adapt itself to music, because its mood is already established. It is the business of the composer to create music which will supplement the poem. A lullaby should not have a martial melody, neither should an exhortation to lofty patriotism be given a melody which induces somnolence.

The same sense of fitness must obtain in the accompaniment. The office of the accompaniment is not merely to keep the singer on the pitch. It must help to tell the story by strengthening the mood of the poem. It must not be trivial or insincere, neither must it overwhelm and thus draw the attention of the listeners to itself and away from the singer.

The accompaniment is the clothing, or dress, of the melody. Melodies, like people, should be well dressed but not over dressed. Some melodies, like some people, look better in plain clothes than in a fancy costume. Other melodies appear to advantage in a rich costume. Modern songwriters are much inclined to overdress their melodies to the extent that the accompaniment forces itself upon the attention to the exclusion of the melody. Such writing is as incongruous as putting on a dress suit to go to a fire.

The significance of the theme should indicate the nature of the accompaniment. To take a simple sentiment and overload [84]it with a modern complex harmonic accompaniment is like going after sparrows with a sixteen inch siege gun.

Comedy in the song should not be associated with tragedy in the accompaniment. A lively poem should not have a lazy accompaniment. The great songwriters were models in this respect. This accounts for their greatness. Take for example Schubert's *Wohin* and *Der Wanderer*, Schumann's *Der Nussbaum*, Brahms' *Feldeinsamkeit*. These accompaniments are as full of mood as either poem or melody.

The element of proportion enters into songwriting no less than into architecture. A house fifteen by twenty feet with a tower sixty feet high and a veranda thirty feet wide would be out of proportion. A song with sixty-four measures of introduction and sixteen measures for the voice would be out of proportion. Making a song is similar to painting a landscape. In the painting the grass, flowers, shrubbery etc., are in the foreground, then come the hills and if there be a mountain range it is in the background. If the mountain range were in the foreground it would obscure everything else. So in making a song. If it tells a story and reaches a climax the climax should come near the end of the song. When the singer has carried his audience with him up to a great emotional height then all it needs is to be brought back safely and quickly to earth and left there.

ASSOCIATION

I have mentioned the principles of song construction, but there are other things which have to do with making a song effective. One of the most important of these is association. Let us remember that the effect and consequent value of music depends upon the class of emotions it awakens rather than upon the technical skill of the composer, and that these emotions are [85]dependent to a considerable extent upon association. We all remember the time honored expedient of tying a string around a finger when a certain thing is to be remembered. The perception of the digital decoration recalls the reason for it and thus the incident is carried to a successful conclusion. In like manner feelings become associated with ideas. Church bells arouse feelings of reverence and devotion. To many of us a brass band awakens pleasant memories of circus day. *Scots Wha Hae* fills the Scotchman with love for his native heather. The odor of certain flowers is offensive because we associate it with a sad occasion. The beauty of a waltz is due not only to its composition but also to our having danced to it under particularly pleasant circumstances.

At the opera there are many things that combine to make it a pleasant occasion—the distant tuning of the orchestra, the low hum of voices, the faint odor of violets, and the recollection of having been there before with that miracle of a girl,—all combine to fill us with pleasurable anticipation. In this way we give as much to the performance as it gives to us. According to some Aestheticians the indefinable emotions we sometimes feel when listening to music are the reverberations of feelings experienced countless ages ago. This may have some foundation in fact, but it is somewhat like seeing in a museum a mummy of ourselves in a previous incarnation.

Songs which have the strongest hold upon us are those which have been in some way associated with our experience. The intensity with which such songs as *Annie Laurie, Dixie, The Vacant Chair, Tramp, Tramp, Tramp* grip us is due almost entirely to association.

Therefore the value of a song consists not alone in what it awakens in the present, but in what it recalls from the past. Man is the sum of his experience; and to make past experience contribute to the joy of the present is to add abundance to riches.

86

VIII
HOW TO STUDY A SONG

The accent of truth apparent in the voice when speaking naturally is the basis of expression in singing.

Garcia. *Hints on Singing.*

First determine the general character of the song. A careful study of the words will enable the student to find its general classification. It may be dramatic, narrative, reminiscent, introspective, contemplative, florid, sentimental.

The following are examples:

Dramatic, *The Erl King*, Schubert.

Narrative, *The Two Grenadiers*, Schumann.

Reminiscent, *Der Doppelgänger*, Schubert.

Florid, *Indian Bell Song*, from Lakme, Delibes.

Introspective, *In der Frühe*, Hugo Wolf.

Contemplative, *Feldeinsamkeit*, Brahms.

Songs of sentiment. This includes all songs involving the affections and the homely virtues.

To these might be added songs of exaltation, such as Beethoven's "Nature's Adoration." Character songs, in which the singer assumes a character and expresses its sentiments. A good example of this is "The Poet's Love" cycle by Schumann. Classifying the song in this way is the first step toward discovering its atmosphere. There is always one tempo at which a song sounds best and this tempo must grow out of a thorough understanding of its character. Metronome marks should be unnecessary. Intelligent study of a song will unerringly suggest the proper tempo.

Next, study the poem until it creates the mood. Read it, not once, but many times. Imbibe not only its intellectual but its emotional content. It is the office of poetry to stimulate 87the imagination. It is under the influence of this stimulus that songs are written, and under its influence they must be sung. Hugo Wolf said that he always studied the poem until it composed the music. This means that he studied the poem until he was so filled with its mood that the proper music came of itself. Fix in mind the principal points in the poem and the order in which they occur. There usually is development of some kind in a poem. Learn what it is. Notice which part of the poem contains the great or central idea. Read it aloud. Determine its natural accent. The singing phrase grows out of the spoken phrase. Singing is elongated, or sustained, speech, but it should be none the less intelligent by reason of this.

Now adapt the words to the music. If the music has grown out of the words as it should, it will follow the development of the poem and give it additional strength.

By this time one should be in the mood of the song, and he should not emerge from it until the song is finished. If one is filled with the spirit of the song, is sincere and earnest, and is filled with a desire to express what is beautiful and good he will not sing badly even if his voice be ordinary.

The composer may do much toward creating the mood for both singer and listener by means of his introduction. The introduction to a song is not merely to give the singer the pitch. It is for the purpose of creating the mood. It may be reminiscent of the principal theme of the song, it may consist of some fragment of the accompaniment, or any other materials which will tend to create the desired mood.

In the introduction to *Rhein-gold* where Wagner wishes to portray a certain elemental condition he uses 136 measures of the chord of E flat major.

In *Feldeinsamkeit* (The Quiet of the Fields) where the mood is such as would come to one lying in the deep grass in the field 88watching "the fair white clouds ride slowly overhead," in a state of complete inaction, Brahms establishes the mood by this treatment of the major chord.

In *Der Wanderer* (The Wanderer) Schubert uses this musical figure to indicate the ceaseless motion of one condemned to endless wandering.

In *The Maid of the Mill* cycle where the young miller discovers the brook Schubert uses this figure, which gives a clear picture of a chattering brooklet. This figure continues throughout the song.

In the song *On the Journey Home*, which describes the feelings of one who, after a long absence returns to view the "vales and mountains" of his youth, Grieg, with two measures of introduction grips us with a mood from which we cannot escape.

89But one of the most striking examples of the operation of genius is Schubert's introduction to *Am Meer* (By the Sea). Here with two chords he tells us the story of the lonely seashore, the deserted hut, the tears, the dull sound of breakers dying on a distant shore, and all around the unfathomable mystery of the mighty deep.

Classic song literature is full of interesting examples of this kind. If we learn how to study the works of these great ones of the earth we shall see how unerring is the touch of genius, and some day we shall awaken to see that these kings and prophets are our friends, and that they possess the supreme virtue of constancy.

90

IX

SCIENTIFIC VOICE PRODUCTION

The immediate effect of the laryngoscope was to throw the whole subject into almost hopeless confusion by the introduction of all sorts of errors of observation, each claiming to be founded on ocular proof, and believed in with corresponding obstinacy.

Sir Morell Mackenzie. *Hygiene of the Vocal Organs.*

He who studies the voice in a physics laboratory naturally considers himself a scientific man, and those teachers who make his discoveries the basis of their teaching believe they are teaching the science of voice production. The scientist says: "Have I not studied the voice in action? I have seen, therefore I know." But the element of uncertainty in what he has seen makes his knowledge little more than speculative. But suppose he is sure of what he has seen. Of what importance is it? He has seen a vocal organ in the act of producing tone under trying conditions, for one under the conditions necessary to the use of the laryngoscope is not at all likely to reach his own standard of tone production.

Scientists would have us believe that the action of the vocal mechanism is the same in all voices. This claim must necessarily be made or there would be no such thing as scientific production. But of all the vocal vagaries advanced this has the least foundation in fact.

Scientifically and artistically speaking there is no such thing at present as perfect voice, and there will be no such thing until man manifests a perfect mind. The best examples of voice production are not altogether perfect, and most of them are still a considerable distance from perfection. It is with these imperfect models that the scientific man in dealing and on which he bases his deductions.

Be it right or wrong singers do not all use the vocal mechanism in the same way. I have in mind two well known contraltos one of whom carried her chest register up to A, and even 91to B flat occasionally. The other carried her middle register down to the bottom of the voice. Can the tenor who carries his chest voice up to   be said to use his voice in the same way as one who begins his head voice at ?

In the examination of a hundred voices selected at random all manner of different things would be observed. Perhaps this is responsible for the great diversity of opinion among scientists, for it must be said that so far there is little upon which they agree. Before absolute laws governing any organ or instrument can be formulated the nature of the instrument must be known. The scientists have never come anywhere near an agreement as to what kind of an instrument man has in his throat. They have not decided whether it is a stringed instrument, a brass, a single or double reed, and these things are vital in establishing a scientific basis of procedure. Not knowing what the instrument is, it is not strange that we are not of one mind as to how it should be played upon.

If we are to know the science of voice production we must first know the mechanism and action of the vocal organ. This instrument, perhaps an inch and a half in length, produces tones covering a compass, in rare instances, of three octaves. How does it do it? According to the books, in a variety of ways.

A majority of those voice teachers who believe in registers recognize three adjustments, chest middle, and upper, or chest medium, and head, but Dr. MacKenzie claims that in four hundred female voices which he examined he found in most cases the chest mechanism was used

32

throughout. Mancini (1774) says there are instances in which there is but one register used throughout.

Garcia says there are three mechanisms—chest, falsetto, and head, and makes them common to both sexes.

92Behnke divides the voice into five registers—lower and upper thick, lower and upper thin, and small.

Dr. Guilmette says that to hold that all of the tones of the voice depend on one mechanism or register is an acknowledgment of ignorance of vocal anatomy. He further declares that the vocal cords have nothing to do with tone—that it is produced by vibration of the mucous membrane of the trachea, larynx, pharynx, mouth; in fact, all of the mucous membrane of the upper half of the body.

When it comes to the falsetto voice, that scarehead to so many people who have no idea what it is, but are morally sure it is wicked and ungodly, the scientists give their imaginations carte blanche. Dr. Mackenzie, who says there are but two mechanisms, the long and short reed, says the falsetto is produced by the short reed.

Lehfeldt and Muller hold that falsetto is produced by the vibrations of the inner edges or mucous covering of the vocal cords, the body of the cords being relaxed.

Mr. Lunn feels sure that the true vocal cords are not involved in falsetto, that voice being produced by the false vocal cords.

Mantels says that in the falsetto voice the vocal cords do not produce pitch, that the quality and mechanism are both that of the flute, that the cords set the air in vibration and the different tones are made by alterations in the length of the tube.

Davidson Palmer says that the falsetto is the remnant of the boy's voice which has deteriorated through lack of use, but which is the correct mechanism to be used throughout the tenor voice.

Mr. Chater argues along the same lines as Mr. Mantels except that he makes the instrument belong to the clarinet or oboe class. Others believe the vocal cords act as the lips do in playing a brass instrument.

93But the action of the vocal cords is but the first part of the unscientific controversy. What takes place above the vocal cords is equally mystifying. The offices of the pharynx, the mouth, the nasal cavities, the entire structure of the head in fact, are rich in uncertainties.

Some think the cavities of the pharynx and head are involved acoustically and in some way enlarge, refine and purify the tone, but one famous man says the head has nothing whatever to do with it. Another gentleman of international reputation says the nose is the most important factor in singing. If your nasal cavities are right you can sing, otherwise you cannot.

And so this verbal rambling continues; so the search for mind in matter goes on, with a seriousness scarcely equalled in any other line of strife. There is nothing more certain to permanently bewilder a vocal student than to deluge him with pseudo-scientific twaddle about the voice. And this for the simple reason that he comes to learn to sing, not for a course in anatomy.

What is scientific voice production? Books without number have been written with the openly expressed intention to give a clear exposition of the subject, but the seeker for a scientific method soon finds himself in a maze of conflicting human opinions from which he cannot extricate himself.

We are told with much unction and warmth that science means to know. That it is a knowledge of principles or causes, ascertained truths or facts. A scientific voice teacher then must know something. What must he know? Books on scientific voice production usually begin with a picture of the larynx, each part of which is labeled with a Greek word sometimes longer than the thing itself. It then proceeds to tell the unction of each muscle and cartilage and the part it plays in 94tone production. Now if this is scientific, and if science is exact knowledge, and this exact knowledge is the basis of scientific voice teaching, then every one who has a perfect knowledge of these facts about the voice, must in the eternal and invariable nature of facts be a perfect voice teacher, and every one of these perfect voice teachers must teach in exactly the same way and produce exactly the same results. Does history support this argument? Quite the reverse.

There is a science of acoustics, and in this science one may learn all about tones, vibrating bodies, vibrating strings, vibrating cavities, simple, compound and complex vibrations. Will this knowledge make him a scientific voice teacher? When he has learned all of this he has not yet begun to prepare for voice teaching. There is no record of a great voice teacher having been trained in a physics laboratory.

It is possible to analyze a tone and learn how fundamental and upper partials are combined and how these combinations affect quality. Does this constitute scientific voice production? This knowledge may all be gained from the various hand books on acoustics. Has any one the hardihood to assert that such knowledge prepares one for the responsible work of training voices? One may know all of this and still be as ignorant of voice training as a Hottentot is of Calvinism.

Further, who shall decide which particular combination of fundamental and upper partials constitutes the perfect singing tone? If a tone is produced and we say, there is the perfect tone, all it proves is that it corresponds to our mental concept of tone. It satisfies our ear, which is another term for our taste.

Can a tone be disagreeable and still be scientifically produced? One combination of fundamental and overtones is, strictly speaking, just as scientific as another combination. The flute tone with its two overtones is just as scientific as the string tone with its six or eight. A tone is pleasant or disagreeable 95according as it corresponds to a mental demand. Even the most hardened scientist would not call a tone which offends his ear scientific. Therefore he must first produce, or have produced the tone that satisfies his ear. The question then naturally arises— when he has secured the tone that satisfies his ear of what value beyond satisfying his curiosity is a physical analysis? A tone is something to hear, and when it satisfies the ear that knows, that in itself is unmistakable evidence that it is rightly produced.

If this scientific knowledge of tone is necessary then every great artist in the world is unscientific, because not one of them makes any use whatsoever of such knowledge in his singing.

No. All of the scientific knowledge one may acquire is no guaranty of success as a teacher, but is rather in the nature of a hindrance, because it is likely to lead him into mechanical ways of doing things. Further, the possession of such knowledge is no indication that one will use it in his teaching. How much of such knowledge can one use in teaching? How can he tell, save from the tone itself whether the pupil is producing it scientifically? It is a well established fact that the more the teacher tries to use his scientific information in teaching the less of an artist he becomes.

Could it be possible that a beautiful tone could be produced contrary to the laws of science? It would be an extraordinary mind that would argue in the affirmative.

The most beautiful tone is the most perfectly produced, whether the singer knows anything of vocal mechanism or not. In such a tone there is no consciousness of mechanics or scientific laws. The vocal mechanism is responding automatically to the highest law in the universe—the law of beauty. The most scientific thing possible is a96beautiful idea perfectly expressed, because a thing inherently beautiful is eternally true, hence it is pure science.

Every tone of the human voice is the expression of life, of an idea, a feeling, an emotion, and unless interfered with the vocal mechanism responds automatically.

He who by experiment or reading has learned the action of the vocal mechanism, and attempts to make his pupil control every part of it by direct effort may imagine that he is teaching scientific voice production, but he is not, he is only doing a mechanical thing in a clumsy way.

Is it a scientific act to tell a pupil to hold his tongue down, as one writer argued recently? Is a teacher calling into action the eternal laws of science when he tells his pupil to drive the tone through the head, hoist the soft palate, groove the tongue, and make the diaphragm rigid? No. He is simply doing a mechanical thing badly for want of a better way. It is no more scientific than kicking the cat out of the way if she gets under your feet.

Any one who has learned the elements of psychology or philosophy knows that everything exists first as idea. The real universe is the one that exists in the mind of the creator. The real man is the part of him that thinks. To hold that the body thinks or acts is equivalent to saying that Gray's "Elegy" was in the pen with which the poet wrote.

To a natural scientist the only real thing is what he can see, therefore he bases his faith on what he conceives to be matter; but if we study the great ones—Oswald, Huxley, Grant, Allen, and the like, we find that they have long ago reached the conclusion that there is no such thing as matter. According to Schopenhauer the world is idea, and this so called material environment is thought objectifying itself.

Vocal teachers, like the members of other professions, are not altogether immune to an attack of intellect, and at such 97times the thought that they are doing something scientific is particularly agreeable.

The only study of science that can benefit any one is the study of causation, and causation cannot be cognized by the physical senses. We never see, hear, feel, taste, or smell cause. What we see or hear is effect. Causation is mental. Natural science is dealing with phenomena, with effect not cause. A regular recurrence of phenomena may establish a so called natural law, but the law is that which caused the phenomena, "Law is force" says Hegel, and it is therefore mental. We are told that the law of the earth is its path around the sun. This is not true, the law of the earth is the mind which makes it revolve around the sun. If we would learn the nature, activity,

34

and cause of anything we must look for it in *mind* not in matter. For this reason the process of voice production is *psychologic* not physiologic. When a pupil sings, what we hear is *effect* not cause. If he is doing all manner of unnecessary things with his lips, tongue, larynx, etc. what we see is effect and the cause is in wrong *mental* concepts. The thing which caused the tone is *mental*, the force which produced it is *mental*, and the means by which we know whether it is good, or bad is *mental.*

Of this we may be sure, that the tone the pupil sings will not be better than the one he has in mind. *A tone exists first as a mental concept, and the quality of the mental concept determines the quality of the tone.*

If there be such a thing as scientific voice production it will be found in the sense of what is inherently beautiful, and the scientific tone is one which will perfectly express a right idea or emotion, and in the nature of things there is an appropriate tone for everything that may be legitimately expressed, for they are correlated ideas.

Whence originated this so called scientific voice teaching? 98That the old Italian knew nothing of it is well understood. They considered the process artistic rather than scientific. *How does it sound*, was their slogan. The thing uppermost in their minds was beautiful tone, and they were wise enough to know that when one has a definite concept of the pure singing tone he has a more valuable asset than all the mechanical knowledge he can acquire. They had but one end in view, namely, a finished artist, and everything they did was made to contribute to it. The artist always has in mind the *finished product*. The scientist tries to find out *how it is done*. The artist begins with the idea and works forward to its complete expression. The scientist begins with the physical mechanism and works backward toward the idea.

What is responsible for the change from the methods of the the seventeenth and eighteenth centuries? It is safe to say that it did not come through the voice teachers.

In the early part of the nineteenth century an interesting thing happened. How it happened or why it happened at that particular time is not known nor does it matter. The human mind became all at once aggressively inquisitive. The desire to get at the ultimate of everything took possession of humanity and still holds it. The result was an era of scientific analysis and invention, the aim of which was to control the forces of nature. Previous to that time methods of living, production, transportation, agriculture, etc. were little different from that of biblical times. People and nations lived much to themselves. They looked within for their inspiration and developed their own national characteristics. But with the invention of the steamship, railway, and telegraph a change came. These improved methods of transportation and communication brought all of the mentalities of the world together, and soon all habitable parts of the globe were in daily and hourly contact. The result was a mental fermentation which increased the complexity 99of civilization immeasurably and the present exaggerated and unnatural condition of society is the outgrowth.

Between 1809 and 1813 were born Mendelssohn, Chopin, Schumann, Liszt, and Wagner. These men are known as the founders of the modern romantic school of music. They grew up with the new civilization and could not do otherwise than reflect its complexity in their music. That the new civilization was responsible for the new art there is no doubt whatever. All old types have passed away. All branches of art have suffered radical changes in conforming to new ideals.

Since the wave of scientific investigation started around the world nothing has been able to escape it. The hand of the scientist has been upon everything, and to him rather than to the voice teachers must be given the credit for originating scientific voice teaching.

When the scientists began publishing the results of their investigations voice teachers at once became interested. The plan looked promising. It offered them a method shorn of uncertainties. A method that brought everything under the operation of physical laws; a method that dealt only with finalities, and would operate in spite of a lack of musical intelligence on the part of the student, and at the same time enable them to lay to their souls the flattering unction of science. True it ignored altogether the psychology of the matter. It said "do it this way and a beautiful tone will come whether you are thinking it or not, because scientific laws eternally operating in the same way eternally produce the same results."

The scientific method gave voice teachers an opportunity to work with something tangible, something they could see; whereas the development of tone concept, the artistic instinct, musical feeling, and musicianship had to do with things which to most of them were intangible and elusive. No one doubts the honesty of the teachers who became obsessed with the100scientific idea. To them it meant increased efficiency and accuracy, quicker results with less effort, and so they broke with the old Italians, the basis of whose teaching was beautiful tone and beautiful singing. In spite of the honesty of purpose of all those who followed the new way, the results were calamitous. The art of singing received a serious setback. Voices without number were ruined. From the middle to the end of the nineteenth century the scientific idea was rampant, and during that period it is probable that the worst voice teaching in the history of the world was done. Large numbers of people with neither musicianship nor musical instincts acquired a smattering of anatomy and a few mechanical rules and advertised themselves as teachers of scientific voice production. The great body of vocal students, anxious to learn to sing in the shortest possible time, having no way of telling the genuine from the spurious except by trying it, fell an easy prey, and the amount of vocal damage and disaster visited upon singers in the name of science is beyond calculation.

Fortunately the reaction has begun. Slowly but surely we are returning to a saner condition of mind. Every year adds to the number of those who recognize singing as an art, whose vision is clear enough to see that the work of the scientific investigator should be confined to the laboratory and that it has no place in the studio. We are beginning to see that the basic principle of singing is *freedom in the expression of the beautiful*, and that the less there is of the mechanical in the process the better.

101

19631668R00023

Printed in Great Britain
by Amazon